Teaching Handbook
Reception/Primary 1

Laura Sharp

Nikki Elliston

Hero Academy Team

Series editors: Paul Stewart and Chris Riddell

Series advisor: Laura Sharp

Guided reading consultant: Nikki Elliston

Curriculum matching: Rachel Russ

Levelling consultant: Catherine Baker

Character illustrations: Bill Ledger

The publisher wishes to thank the following schools for their valuable contribution to the trialling and development of this series: Hughenden Primary School, High Wycombe; St. Mary's CEP School, Rawtenstall; Ipplepen Primary School, Ipplepen; Kings Heath Primary School, Birmingham; Wolvercote Primary School, Oxford; East Oxford Primary School, Oxford; Kidmore End Primary School, Reading; Pegasus Primary School, Oxford; Belmont Primary School, Erith; Grosvenor Road Primary, Manchester; Stanton Harcourt CE Primary School, Witney; Longfleet Primary School, Poole; Hurlingham School, London; Earlsheaton Infants School, Dewsbury; Bede Burn Primary, Jarrow Tyne and Wear; St. Helen's Church of England Primary School, Rochester; Holy Family Catholic Primary School, Blackpool; Dial Park Primary School, Stockport; Mengham Infant School, Hayling Island; St Christopher's C of E School, Langford; Brookside Primary School, Bicester.

OXFORD
UNIVERSITY PRESS

Great Clarendon Street, Oxford, OX2 6DP,
United Kingdom

Oxford University Press is a department of the University of Oxford.
It furthers the University's objective of excellence in research, scholarship,
and education by publishing worldwide. Oxford is a registered trade mark of
Oxford University Press in the UK and in certain other countries

© Oxford University Press 2018

The moral rights of the author have been asserted

First Edition published in 2018

British Library Cataloguing in Publication Data

Data available

978-0-19-841687-6

3 5 7 9 10 8 6 4

Paper used in the production of this book is a natural, recyclable product
made from wood grown in sustainable forests. The manufacturing process conforms
to the environmental regulations of the country of origin.

Printed in Great Britain by Bell and Bain Ltd, Glasgow

Acknowledgements
Illustrations by Bill Ledger
Photo assets supplied by shutterstock.com, cgtrader.com, turbosquid.com.

Contents

Welcome to Hero Academy!

Hero Academy is a series of highly motivating books set around a school for superheroes. These fully decodable, finely-levelled stories can be used flexibly in the classroom for independent, one-to-one, or guided reading sessions to inspire all young readers.

Hero Academy is brought to you by the creators of Project X

Project X is an engaging and effective reading and writing programme published by Oxford University Press.

Project X is developed by the very best educational experts and provides teaching and learning resources explicitly designed to support boys and address the gender gap in literacy.

Effective whole-school guided reading (Reception/Primary 1–Year 6/Primary 7)

Decodable independent reading adventures (Reception/Primary 1–Year 6/Primary 7)

A proven phonics intervention (Year 2/Primary 3–Year 4/Primary 5)

Comprehension success in 10 weeks (Year 4/Primary 5–Year 6/Primary 7)

Writing skills development in an interactive world (Reception/Primary 1–Year 6/Primary 7)

Phonics practice to embed learning (Reception/Primary 1–Year 1/Primary 2)

*Primary/P references in this handbook relate to Primary year groups in Scotland and Northern Ireland.

Series overview

Reading books

Hero Academy is a school where anything can and does happen! Join the pupils as they learn to control their powers, battle with baddies, and help protect their school and Lexis City.

The series comprises 78 thrilling stories, with a cast of memorable heroes and unforgettable villains. In Reception/Primary 1, the adventures are based around the academy itself. Readers will appreciate the characters' superpowers while recognizing that the heroes have lessons, learn new skills, make mistakes, and have fun with their friends – just like they do. As with any school, sometimes things don't go as planned!

All the books in the series are **carefully levelled** and correlate to Oxford Levels and Book Bands, so you can quickly and easily help your pupils choose books that are at the right reading level for them.

Hero Academy is **fully decodable** and reflects the reading requirements of the Statutory Frameworks for the Early Years Foundation Stage (EYFS) and the English Curriculum for Key Stage 1 and 2. For more information about how **Hero Academy** supports the Scottish Curriculum for Excellence, the Foundation Phase Framework in Wales, and the Northern Ireland Curriculum, see pages 114–124. The series follows a systematic synthetic phonics structure and correlates to *Letters and Sounds* Phases 1–6. The small steps of phonic progression allow children in Reception/Primary 1 the chance to practise and consolidate their phonics skills and ensure they become fluent, accurate and enthusiastic readers. The phonic phase and common/high-frequency words can be found on the back covers of each book and are summarized in the structure chart in this handbook.

As well as the effective implementation of a systematic phonics programme, one of the key recommendations of the Education Endowment Foundation report for improving literacy in Key Stage 1 (KS1) is to use a balanced and engaging approach to developing reading skills, which helps children to 'develop persistence and resilience as well as enjoyment and satisfaction in their reading'[1].

Hero Academy offers interesting, innovative storylines with plenty of opportunities for discussion or 'book talk'. Giving children the chance to talk about what they have read can significantly enhance their understanding. Consequently, pupils cumulatively build up their reading confidence, becoming engaged and enthusiastic readers who *can* and *will* read independently for enjoyment. Comprehension support is integrated into the inside cover notes in each book and is provided throughout this handbook.

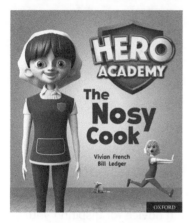

---

[1] Education Endowment Foundation, 2017. *Improving Literacy in Key Stage One*, London: Education Endowment Foundation.

The Companions

The **Hero Academy** Companions are perfect for hooking children into the series as they provide lots of background information about the heroes and villains, along with extra story comic strips and things to make and do. They can be used as a springboard for writing activities, and can generate talk in pairs, groups or with the whole class.

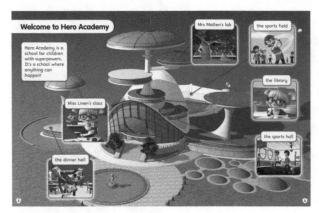

The Handbooks

In each of the **Hero Academy** Handbooks, you will find advice for inspiring your young reading heroes and support for independent and guided reading. Also included is comprehension, phonics and levelling progression, assessment guidance, and photocopiable masters for each reading book in the series, plus lots of fun extras.

Oxford Owl is an award-winning website supporting children's learning at school and at home. *Oxford Owl for School* provides free online teaching, learning and assessment resources, expert support and subscriptions for primary schools. Register free to join a community of other teachers at: www.oxfordowl.co.uk

About our series editors

Chris Riddell

Chris Riddell is the creator of an extraordinary range of books which have won many illustration awards including the UNESCO Prize, the Greenaway Medal (on three occasions) and the Hay Festival Medal for Illustration. His work includes *Ottoline* titles, and the Goth Girl series, the first book of which won the Costa Children's Book Award. Chris has also achieved global success through his New York Times best-selling collaboration on *The Edge Chronicles* with Paul Stewart and through his illustrated works with other high-profile figures including Neil Gaiman and the comedian Russell Brand. Chris was the Waterstones Children's Laureate 2015–2017 and was appointed Book Trust's first official ambassador in 2017. He lives and works in Brighton.

Paul Stewart

Paul Stewart is an international star who has written everything from travel writing to football stories, fantasy and horror. His collaboration with Chris Riddell on The Edge Chronicles has taken him to bestseller lists in both the UK and USA. A graduate of Lancaster University and of the University of East Anglia's creative writing course, Paul travelled for many years and has travelled extensively throughout Europe, the Indian sub-continent, the Far East, Australasia, North America and East Africa. He lived in Germany and Sri Lanka, teaching English as a foreign language, before returning to England and subsequently becoming a full-time writer. Paul has a grown-up son and daughter, and lives with his wife in Brighton.

Hero Academy structure chart

Year Group	Oxford Level	Book Band		Book no.**	Book Title	Letters and Sounds Phase	Companions	Teachers' Resource
Reception/Primary 1*	1	Lilac	A	1	Cat Chase	Phase 1	Companion 1	Reception/ Primary 1 Teaching Handbook
				2	Jin Can Fly			
			B	3	The Lost Cat	Phase 2, Set 1		
				4	Jin's First Day			
	1+	Pink	A	5	Pip's Prank	Phase 2, Set 2		
				6	It is a Tip!			
			B	7	Cat in a Cap	Phase 2, Set 3		
				8	Stop, Cat!			
			C	9	Tuck In	Phase 2, Set 4		
				10	Magnus is Stuck			
			D	11	Jin is Ill	Phase 2, Set 5		
				12	Ben Helps			
	2	Red	A	13	Jin Lifts Off	Phase 3, Set 6		
				14	Will the Reds Win?			
			B	15	The Zipbot	Phase 3, Set 7		
				16	Pip's Mess			
			C	17	Slink's Snack	Phase 3		
				18	Fix That Bell!			
	3	Yellow	A	19	It is Freezing			
				20	Win the Cup!			
			B	21	Turnip is Missing	Phase 3		
				22	Zoom Food			
			C	23	Stuck in the Storm			
				24	The Fizzing Mixture			
Year 1/Primary 2	4	Light Blue	A	25	The Pest			Year 1/ Primary 2 Teaching Handbook
				26	Ben's Gift			
			B	27	Up, Up, Down	Phase 4		
				28	Flag Down!			
			C	29	Digger on the Run			
				30	Baa-Beep!			
	5	Green	A	31	Monster Sprouts			
				32	Ben to the Rescue			
			B	33	Stuck to the Ice	Phase 5		
				34	The Boostertron			
			C	35	The Super Glooper			
				36	Attack of the Robot Bunnies			
	6	Orange	A	37	The Nosy Cook			
				38	Professor Bounce			
			B	39	Ice Crystal Robbery	Phase 5		
				40	The Protecto			
			C	41	Invasion of the Bunny-wunnies			
				42	Dancing Danger			

Year Group	Oxford Level	Book Band	Book no.	Book Title	Letters and Sounds Phase	Companions	Teachers' Resource
Year 2/Primary 3	7	Turquoise	43	The Exagger-tron	Phase 6	Companion 2	Year 2/ Primary 3 Teaching Handbook
			44	Bug Alert!			
			45	Cake Chaos			
			46	Super Coldo			
			47	Bunny-wunny Bank Raid			
			48	Attack of the Chomping Nibblers			
	8	Purple	49	Power Swap	Phase 6		
			50	Out of Control			
			51	Doctor Daze and the Bamboozler			
			52	Mr Gleam			
			53	Stop that Mammoth!			
			54	Silver Shadow			
	9	Gold	55	The Champion's Cup	Phase 6		
			56	Super Coldo's Revenge			
			57	Night Rescue			
			58	The Pea-souper			
			59	False Alarms			
			60	Silver Shadow Strikes Again			
	10	White	61	Calling All Villains!	Phase 6		
			62	Demolition Danger			
			63	Operation Bubble Wrap			
			64	Blast from the Past			
			65	The Superpower Games			
			66	The Super-strength Trials			
	11	Lime	67	Bunny-wunny Blockade	N/A		
			68	Doctor Nowhere			
			69	Operation Poach			
			70	The Mysterious Miss Tula			
			71	Mr Squid's Revenge			
			72	Robo-hop			
	12	Lime +	73	Catnapped	N/A		
			74	Race for the Meteorite			
			75	A Major Shock			
			76	The Termite-nator			
			77	Code Red!			
			78	Villain Academy			

*Primary/P

Primary/P references in this handbook relate to Primary year groups in Scotland and Northern Ireland.

**Book numbers

Book numbers are given here for teacher reference only to reflect the small steps of progression in the **Hero Academy** series. The books themselves are not numbered and can be read in any order (depending on the level the pupil is reading at).

Enrol your pupils into Hero Academy!

The overarching theme of superheroes in this series taps into children's imagination and enthusiasm. Importantly, it is a theme that's motivating for boys who are starting out on their reading journey and in developing the habit of reading for pleasure.

In order to introduce **Hero Academy** to your class and stimulate pupils' interest in the new characters, consider the following …

- Have a hero-themed registration, e.g. ask children to practise their favourite superhero/power pose when their name is called; have themed name badges; or start the day with a superhero quiz or fact.

- Discuss superheroes that children already know. Tease out what heroes have in common: what specific talents, skills or strengths they have; what they wear; what special gadgets and machines they use; how they overcome baddies and make sure everyone is safe.

- Find out what superpowers children would have if they could choose their own and why.

- Show the class the **Hero Academy** Companions, which are perfect for generating talk.

- Show pictures of the characters the children will meet and introduce them. This information can be found in the Companions and on page 2 in the reading books.

- Store the books in a distinctive **Hero Academy** container or place, e.g. a small suitcase, a box with the **Hero Academy** badge on it, or a particular book shelf.

Reading areas (or book corners)

Your class and corridor reading areas are a great starting point for inspiring pupils, and there are many things that you could provide to enhance the theme, spur children's imagination, and encourage lots of speaking and listening around the topic of superheroes. For example:

- Display pictures of the characters they will meet in the books.

- Scribe selected children's comments to add to the display.

- As the pupils progress in their reading of the books, additional information can be displayed alongside the character portraits to build up character profiles.

Remember that reading areas should:

- be comfortable, purposeful spaces that invite participation by pupils,
- be organized, where books are stored for easy retrieval,
- be regularly reviewed and updated with the pupils as appropriate,
- reflect current interests of pupils,
- contain focus displays to encourage independent choice,
- evidence children's responses to books and reading: likes, dislikes, favourite books and characters.

Adult modelling of reading area behaviours is particularly important in Reception/Primary 1. This is where you explicitly and implicitly demonstrate to your pupils:

- how reading is a valued activity for all,
- the wide variety of texts – fiction, non-fiction, magazines, comics, catalogues, brochures – that you want the pupils to experience,
- how reading can be an individual or a social, group experience,
- how books are stored and handled for ease of retrieval and return,
- that 'book talk' with others is key to reading enjoyment and to good comprehension of what has been read.

Role play

Role play encourages purposeful speaking and listening between pupils and between adults and pupils. Here are some suggestions of what you could provide or make:

- simple cloaks or vests in a variety of colours to indicate the different hero characters – make a smaller one for Slink! These can be made from fabric or old t-shirts with the arms cut off and the front cut down. If you don't have the fabric available, you could ask children to put on their own 'invisible' cloak every time they read a **Hero Academy** story,
- **Hero Academy** name badges to attach to costumes – see the *Hero Academy name badges* photocopiable master (page 13),
- a set of ears and a collar for Slink – see the *Slink (Combat Cat)* photocopiable master (page 14),
- individual masks can be made using a basic template – see the *Superhero masks* photocopiable master (page 15),
- simple stick puppets to re-enact stories – see the *Simple superhero puppets* photocopiable master (page 16).

Reading superheroes

- Make some 'This superhero is reading' cloaks for your book area or for children to wear in other indoor or outdoor learning areas.

- Get the children to make their own superhero bookmarks – see the *Superhero bookmarks* photocopiable master (page 17).

- Provide badges/cards/medals for good reading, completing a book etc – see the *Reading heroes* photocopiable master (page 38). These could be awarded in a Key Stage or whole-school assembly as recognition of children's emerging reading skills. They could be mentioned in a regular home-school newsletter, or recorded and displayed in a special assembly book. This will act as a key motivator to keep children on their reading journey.

See *Feedback on reading* (pages 35–36) for advice on giving feedback in Reception.

Hero Academy name badges

Teacher notes

Photocopy the character name badges below on to card. Introduce them to pupils as they meet the characters in the **Hero Academy** stories. Attach a simple fastener to the back of the badges. Children can choose which character they will be during role play or while reading. Keep the badges in a special container in the reading area or role play area. There are blank name badges for other character names they come across, or children could make their own superhero name badge.

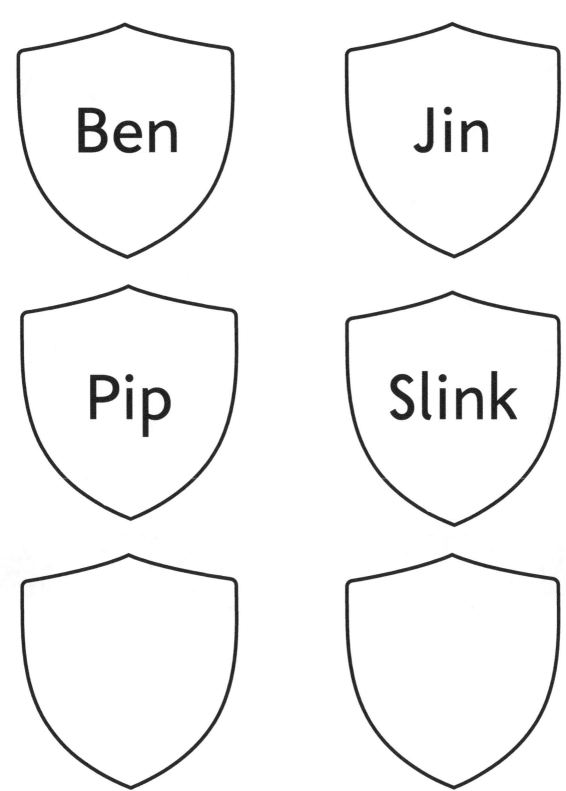

Slink (Combat Cat)

Teacher notes

Photocopy the ear and collar shapes below on to card. Cut them out and ask children to decorate them. Help children to attach the ears to a child's headband. Make the collar fastening using a paper fastener. Children can then wear them when they're reading a book about Slink (Combat Cat) or role playing being the superhero cat.

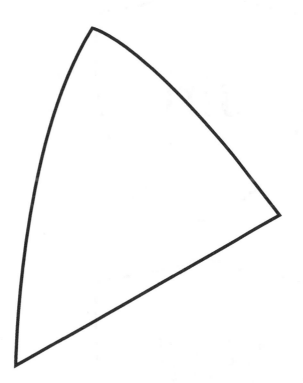

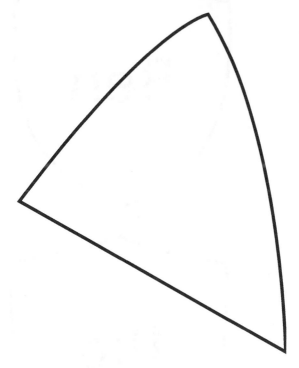

Superhero masks

Teacher notes

Photocopy the mask templates below on to card or trace them on to felt fabric, and ask children to decorate them. Fasten using elastic.

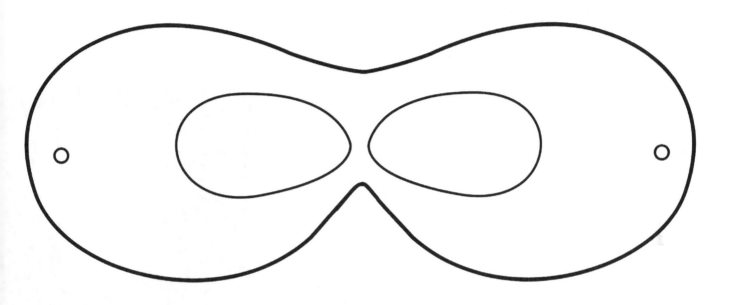

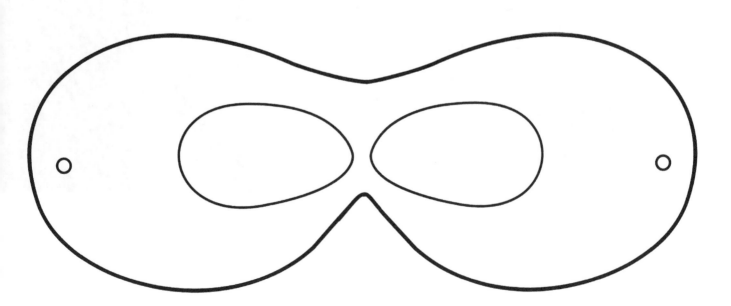

Simple superhero puppets

Teacher notes

Stick puppets of the characters encourage children to re-enact the stories, thus helping their recall, sequencing and comprehension. They could record their retellings of the stories using a digital camera or tablet.

- Use the images below as a starting point for the puppets, and attach them to lolly sticks, straws or cardboard rolls.
- Alternatively, use a wooden spoon as the figure shape. Children could draw the face of their favourite character on to the spoon, or you could photocopy the character faces below and glue them on. Paint the main costume colours on the spoon handle. Add fabric/paper detail.

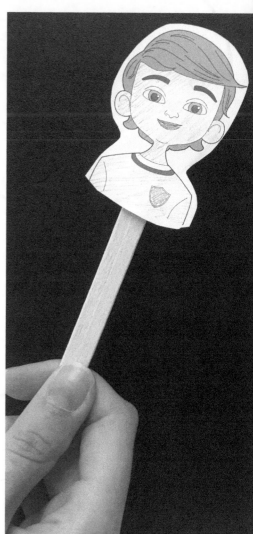

HERO ACADEMY

Superhero bookmarks

Teacher notes

Photocopy the bookmark templates below on to thick card. Ask children to colour them in. A thick rubber band or piece of elastic can be added to secure the bookmark to the book.

Name: ....

I can *Boost* my reading
with Pip!

Name: ....

Swoop into a book
with Jin!

Name: ....

Have a reading *Sprint*
with Ben!

Name: ....

Curl up and read with
Combat Cat!

The reading process

The journey to independence

Learning to read is a long and multifaceted journey, and the ultimate destination is to ensure that children become independent readers who:

- read often,
- read for a variety of purposes,
- choose to read for pleasure and for information,
- actively engage with the process of learning to read,
- are motivated to read widely from a range of texts of increasing challenge and complexity.

In Reception/Primary 1, children are just embarking on their reading journey, so we need to ensure a positive experience from the outset providing:

- a purposeful and engaging environment,
- quality reading materials for consolidation of what children know and can do,
- a clear approach for explicit teaching of reading skills based on children's learning needs,
- plenty of opportunities to practise and consolidate new knowledge and skills and apply them in other areas of learning,
- opportunities to listen to good texts read aloud, i.e. adults modelling what 'good readers' do.

> *There is a broad consensus, supported by research evidence, that reading requires both decoding and comprehension... It is also important to remember that progress requires motivation and engagement.*[1]

Phonics

The Alphabetic Code is a route map to knowing the letters on the page represent the sounds in spoken words, i.e. grapheme-phoneme correspondence.

Children need to 'crack' the Alphabetic Code in order to read words on the page. It needs to be taught regularly and systematically from Reception/Primary 1 through the explicit teaching of phonics. Children should incrementally build up their phonic knowledge of graphemes and the speech sound(s) they represent and practise the skill of blending the sounds *all through the word* to read. This should be taught as the prime approach for decoding unfamiliar words.

As words are repeatedly encountered, children should be expected to read words without overt sounding out or 'undue hesitation'. The goal is to develop speed of accurate reading (fluency) so that decoding becomes automatic. This in turn supports comprehension of what has been read.

> The **Hero Academy** books have been written to reflect a clear teaching progression, based on *Letters and Sounds*, which will complement your systematic synthetic phonics programme. See pages 43–47 for a full phonic breakdown of the stories in Reception/Primary 1 .

[1] Education Endowment Foundation, 2017. *Improving Literacy in Key Stage One*, London: Education Endowment Foundation.

Common exception words

Some words—common exception words, or tricky words—are not completely phonically decodable at the early stages of learning, e.g. *the, said*. However, these words occur regularly in texts and support the independent reading of simple sentences right from the outset. Children need to be taught to read these words; this requires repeated practice for the words to become familiar and automatically read. These words are introduced progressively in the **Hero Academy** stories within the context of fully punctuated sentences. The order of their introduction is on *Phonic and vocabulary overview* pages (pages 43-47).

Comprehension

Independent readers not only decode words on a page, they seek out meaning. They understand what they have read and are not satisfied with 'non-comprehension'. In the early stages of learning to read, we need to provide teaching that will address both components of decoding and comprehension. This is reflected in Early Years Foundation Stage Profile 2018 handbook, ELG 9. *'Children read and understand simple sentences. They use phonic knowledge to decode regular words and read them aloud accurately. They also read some common irregular words. They demonstrate understanding when talking with others about what they have read.'*

Early reading comprehension is an active process that requires the child to:

- accurately decode words on the page,
- understand vocabulary,
- engage with the text – making connections to their own knowledge and experience of texts,
- recall and sequence events,
- begin to infer and deduce meaning beyond literal interpretation,
- check their own understanding and seek clarification if needed.

Teachers need to teach children to comprehend through the demonstration of how good readers:

- check their understanding – rereading where necessary,
- activate prior knowledge – make links between what they know and new information,
- make predictions about what will happen and change as necessary as they read on,
- discuss texts with others,
- have a response to or a view on what they are reading.

Through explicit modelling of comprehension skills, teachers introduce children to a repertoire of strategies that they can call on, independently, when reading.

The *Assessment of reading comprehension skills and behaviours chart* on page 108 provides a starting point for collating observations on this vital component in assessing children's reading.

A helpful comprehension mnemonic for one-to-one reading with children

Start. Start with phonics and vocabulary. Can children decode the words fluently and understand what they have read?

Understand. Check children understand key aspects, such as characters, events, titles and information.

Predict. Predict what might happen on the basis of what has been read so far.

Events. Identify and explain the sequence of events in texts.

Read between the lines. Make inferences from the text.

Questioning

Questioning plays a large part in interactions between children and adults and is a skilled task. Teacher questioning requires an element of planning and also the ability to probe children's responses to planned questions.

In Reception/Primary 1, the categories below are generally used; they are loosely based on Bloom's Taxonomy. The categories overlap and are not exclusive of each other but do offer a hierarchy of skills and experiences that build on each other. For example, literal understanding of text is the foundation of the higher-order thinking required to infer meaning from text or evaluate a text.

It should be borne in mind that too many questions can inhibit children's responses, and that too many closed questions that require a 'yes' or 'no' answer can 'close down' children's talk about the text. Adults need to be aware of this and ensure they provide prompts and use ways of opening up discussion.

Question category	Skills and knowledge required from the reader	Example
Literal understanding • tend to be 'closed' questions • reader repeats what the text says	• recall/memory • know that answers are in the text – explicit • find and retrieve text • restate text	• Where does the story take place? • Who did Pip find in the garden? • What was Magnus's pet rat called?
Inferring • 'open' questions but relating closely to the context • go beyond the literal information in the text	• close reading of text required • ability to interpret what is written • activation of some prior knowledge of context • begin to recognize a simple theme • make predictions • begin to monitor their understanding	• Why do you think Ray Ranter said that? • How do you think Jin is feeling now?
Deducing • tend to be 'open' questions • readers draw conclusions based on information given in the text	• draw conclusions about characters and events • use and identify evidence from the text to support ideas • know that evidence builds up through the text • begin to have a sense of author's intent • question their understanding and seek clarification where necessary	• Did your view of Silver Shadow change as the story went on? • What words or phrases in the text made you think that?

Hero Academy books have inside cover notes that help plan for both components of the reading process. They contain:

- suggestions to familiarize children with the text prior to reading,
- words used in the text containing the focus GPCs,
- a list of words that will develop children's vocabulary development and aid their comprehension,
- example questions that can be used to check children's understanding,
- further activities associated with the story.

There are also Guided reading notes, with detailed questions for each book in Reception/Primary 1 (see pages 52–101).

Questioning matrix

Access to a model bank of questions or a question matrix is a useful resource for less experienced teachers and teaching assistants alike. They can take a variety of forms, but the key is to keep it simple and usable, as per the matrix below. Questions of increasing complexity can be constructed using one word from the left-hand column and another from the top row. For example:

- *What is ... Magnus's job at Hero Academy?*
- *Why might ... Slink turn into Combat Cat?*

	>>> Complexity >>>					
	is ... Present	did ... Past	can ... Possibility	would ... Probability	will ... Prediction	might ... Imagination
Who Person						
What Event						
Where Place						
When Time						
Why Reason						
How Meaning						

However you devise questions to lead book talk in your classrooms, it's worth remembering that 'less is more'. Two or three good questions or question prompts are all that is needed to stimulate discussion.

Fluency

Fluency is the ability to read a continuous text automatically, accurately and with appropriate pace and expression either aloud (in the case of beginner readers) or to oneself. It supports comprehension as it allows readers to focus their energies and attention on reading for meaning.

Children need to practise fluent reading regularly right from the start. Through this, they learn how to 'phrase' the text and read with expression and *'sound like a reader'*. The more they do this, the more confident and independent they become.

In the classroom, opportunities should be provided for beginner readers to:

- hear experienced readers modelling expressive and purposeful reading,
- return to and reread known texts,
- take part in 'echo reading', where the child repeats what a more experienced reader has just read,
- take part in 'choral reading', where an experienced reader and the child read the text together simultaneously.

Children who need more support

Children start the Reception year with a varying range of reading experiences. For those with less exposure to books, we need to ensure our provision presents learning to read as a positive experience. The majority of these children will not have had experience of a rich language environment in the earliest years. Adult demonstration of book handling skills, being read to, actively participating in a stimulating book area and discussion and activities around books provide a basis for developing those all-important, confident reading attitudes.

Supplementary provision/additional practice may be needed initially in the form of:

- the clear articulation of phonemes,
- the skill of blending phonemes all through an unknown word to decode the word,
- automatic reading of common exception words,
- thorough book overviews to activate prior knowledge and to introduce new vocabulary,
- matching spoken word to printed word (1-1 correspondence),
- taking notice of punctuation,
- choral reading (see **Fluency** on previous page),
- rereading sentences to build up fluency – 'sounding like a reader',
- book talk with an experienced reader on story events, characters and settings.

Provision for children making good progress

Reception teachers need to be constantly alert to each child's pattern of learning and development. Children who have readily-grasped decoding skills are well on their way to being a reader, and it's important to harness the enthusiasm of the successful beginner reader. However, as previously noted, there is more to being a reader than applying phonics to an unknown text. We need to ensure that children are appropriately challenged and supported across the two dimensions of reading – word recognition and language comprehension. A careful balance also needs to be struck between a child's well-honed abilities to read words on a page and subject matter. The content of texts for more advanced readers is not always suitable although the child will be able to decode the words on the page.

Provide opportunities to:

- take part in book talk, which offers a myriad of opportunities for teachers to extend vocabulary and go beyond literal understanding of text, inferring and speculating,
- reflect on reading through a simple reading log of books read in school and home,
- recast their reading as a role play or puppet show for others,
- experience a wide range of texts including non-fiction and poetry,
- talk about authors,
- discuss themes, e.g. defeating villains or finding and using your strengths.

The fine progression of texts in the **Hero Academy** series can support children to access more complex texts with age-appropriate content.

Reading journey record

Periodically have a learning conversation with the child about their journey to becoming a reader. This can take the form of questions to stimulate discussion and encourage children to reflect on their reading. See the *Reading journey record* photocopiable master (page 24). Complete the record together based on the child's reflections. Revisit the statements as appropriate, say three times, throughout the child's time in Reception/Primary 1. This record can be shared/made available to parents/carers, to discuss and complete with their children.

The relationship between guided and independent reading

The finely-levelled **Hero Academy** texts lend themselves to group and guided reading sessions. Guided reading is a key pedagogy for the teacher and an important reading experience for beginner and early readers on their journey to reading independence.

Guided reading:

- is a 'half-way house' for the child between full dependency on support accessing an unknown text and being able to engage with a text independently,
- is an opportunity for the child to synthesize explicitly taught reading strategies, i.e. show what they can do while the teacher observes, guides and prompts (but only where necessary),
- uses texts at instructional level that carefully challenge the reader while building in plenty of opportunities for reading success,
- provides teachers with a rich formative assessment opportunity while observing how children tackle unfamiliar text, thus identifying next steps on the journey to independence,
- emphasizes the 'sociability' and pleasure of reading by the group discussion of the text after reading, thus supporting comprehension.

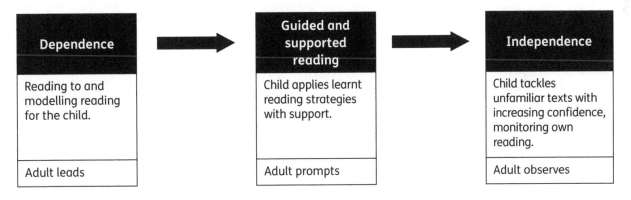

Dependence		**Guided and supported reading**		**Independence**
Reading to and modelling reading for the child.	→	Child applies learnt reading strategies with support.	→	Child tackles unfamiliar texts with increasing confidence, monitoring own reading.
Adult leads		Adult prompts		Adult observes

Guided reading notes are provided for each **Hero Academy** book. See pages 52–101.

Reading journey record

Name: **Date:**

Slink wants to know....

1. Do I enjoy reading?

2. Do I choose to look at and read books on my own?

3. Do I listen attentively to stories, rhymes and poems and join in?

4. Can I say what I think about a story or poem?

5. Can I remember what has happened in a story and tell you about it?

6. Can I say who the characters are in a story?

7. Can I blend sounds all through an unknown word to read it?

8. Can I read words and simple sentences?

9. Can I answer questions about what I have read?

10. Can I tell you what I think might happen in a story?

Activities to support reading (and writing)

In addition to the direct teaching and practising of reading, teachers need to offer activities and experiences to sustain and stimulate children's interest in reading and promote their independence. **Hero Academy** provides a theme that is easily accessible for young children, given that they have just started school themselves – just as the characters in the stories have.

The following play-based suggestions, linked to the themes and characters in **Hero Academy**, can be adapted for both indoor and outdoor provision. They have been devised to offer a variety of learning opportunities to practise and consolidate learning.

Ask me! labels

Occasionally, when children have read a **Hero Academy** book, give them an 'ask me' label, like the example shown (see the *Ask me!* and *Reading heroes* photocopiable masters on pages 37 and 38), to encourage them to talk about what they have read. All adults, including parents and carers, can then start up a conversation where the child is the expert, deciding what is the important element of the story for them. The child can wear the label for the day and one could also be attached to their *Reading journey record* (page 24). These are also referenced for use after the guided reading sessions.

Name:

I'm reading Hero Academy books.

Let's talk about

....

Date:

Story maps

Retelling and sequencing of what has been read is an important early reading skill and requires practice. At Reception/Primary 1, the **Hero Academy** books provide a simple story map on the last page of each book to support this. Encourage children to use these to retell the story to their peers, other adults or reading buddies.

Read aloud again

Rereading known texts builds self-confidence in a reader. This can be rereading to an adult or an older child. Alternatively, children could try using simple digital recording devices, such as tablets; these give another purpose and a different audience, which can be motivating for some children. These recordings can then be shared with others, including parents and carers as appropriate.

You might like to set up an area in the classroom or as part of outdoor provision where children can reread books independently, recording as they do so. A few classroom toys could provide the audience.

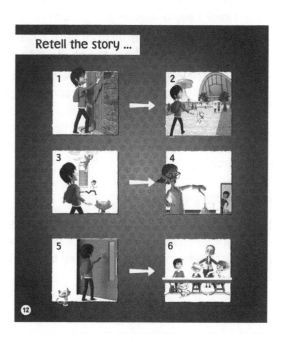

Retell the story ...

Slink's super-vocabulary

Display some words from the *Developing vocabulary* section of the inside cover notes of each **Hero Academy** book in a prominent position in your classroom or reading area. Gradually build up the display. Make sure children understand the meaning of the words. Refer to them regularly and model their use, articulating the words clearly. Ensure children reread them, and encourage children to use the words in their role play and independent writing.

Have a 'Slink thinks' session where children read the word/s that Slink is thinking (see the *Slink thinks* photocopiable master on page 28). Children then say the words aloud and use them in a phrase or sentence – adult modelling of this is important. For example, in the Oxford Level 1+, Pink Book Band story *Pip's Prank*, children begin to understand that a 'prank' means to play a trick on someone, as Pip does to Ben in the story. After seeing the word written down in isolation and articulating the word aloud several times, it begins to be part of the child's known words. Putting the word into self-generated phrases then secures it as part of their working vocabulary.

High-frequency word practice

High-frequency words need lots of practice to be automatically read 'without undue hesitation' (as it states in the National Curriculum in England). This is because it supports fluent reading leading to comprehension as decoding skills and energies are used for unfamiliar words only. Quick recognition comes with regular practice of seeing, reading and saying the word in isolation and in seeing, reading and saying the word within a phrase or sentence.

Sets of simple high-frequency word flashcards can be used for a variety of activities with class, groups or individual children. They can also be adapted for indoor and outdoor provision.

- Set a timer to one minute. Display high-frequency words taught on a chart or on a whiteboard. How many words can be read aloud in that time? Keep a tally as you go. *Can we beat the record another time?*
- Have small individual grids with high-frequency words written on them. Say the word and ask the children to point to the words.
- Near the classroom door, have a box or bag containing multiple copies of high-frequency word flashcards. As children leave for assembly, play or lunchtime, they take a card, read it aloud and then place it in another bag or box. If they can't read it, tell them the word and ask them to say the word clearly. Follow up by showing and asking them the word again that day.

Reading practice

In the early stages of learning to read, children need multiple meaningful opportunities to apply their phonics skills to reading tasks. Decodable short reading texts such as those provided by the **Hero Academy** series are key to this.

Using the *Phonic and vocabulary overview* pages (pages 43–47), additional reading material can be made for consolidation and practice. From Oxford Level 1+, Pink Book Band onward, creating decodable sentences using the **Hero Academy** theme is a playful approach to encouraging wider reading and applying new skills and knowledge. These can be used in a variety of ways to encourage independent reading.

- Have an action or task-related sentence on display for children to decode as they come into class in the morning and after lunch.
- Ask the children to read and then perform the action or task.
- Ask the children to add sound buttons to selected words.
- Cut up the sentence into words and ask children to put it back into a sentence.
- Display the whole sentence. Read it with the children then remove it. Say the sentence with the children. Repeat the sentence as necessary. Then display a range of decodable words including those from the sentence and ask children to read the words and select the words they need to recreate the original sentence.

See the *Decodable sentences* and the *Silly sentences* photocopiable masters on pages 29–32 for some suggestions of sentences.

Response cards

Sometimes children require an extra bit of support to contribute to book discussions. Primarily they may be reticent and lack the confidence to initiate a response or ask a question. Response cards, particularly in a small group, can help overcome that reticence while still keeping the child engaged with the learning intention; the child simply chooses a relevant card and places it in front of them. In this way, the adult can gauge what they might need help with and offer additional support. For example, rephrasing the question or commenting again. The cards should be made up into sets for each child and gradually introduced; they can be added to as children's reading develops. See the *Response cards* photocopiable master (page 33).

Reading partner prompts

Reading partner sessions allow children to share their reading success with others and offer that all-important rereading of known texts. The activity benefits both the reader who gets extra practice and the listener who has to follow the text, keeping pace with the reader. Partners can be from the same class or one pupil can be from an older year group who takes on the role of 'expert reader'. Clear expectations need to be set for the role of reader and listener, and initially adults should model this. Simple reminders of the process could be provided and displayed prominently or provided

as a card to the listener. See the *Reading partners* photocopiable master (page 34).

Slink thinks

Decodable sentences: Oxford Level 1+, Pink Book Band

	✓
1. Pat and tap on the pan.	
2. Ben and Pip sit.	
3. Tip the pan on the mat.	
4. Slink is in a big cap and a top.	
5. Kick the can and pop the cap.	
6. Pick up the rock, Pip.	
7. Go up to Jin and get the jet pack.	
8. Get the mop from Magnus.	
9. Jin will spin and land in a gap.	
10. Pip has no spots on her cap.	

Decodable sentences: Oxford Level 2, Red Book Band

	✓
1. Jin can twist and spin and land on the box.	
2. Pip and Ben bat and get lots of runs.	
3. Jin gets a red vest and jets up.	
4. Ben zigzags across the grass.	
5. Jin spills lots of lemon liquid on the bench.	
6. Slink got a snack of fish, chips and chicken.	
7. Pip will pass the test to ring the bell and win!	
8. Pick up a drink from the lunch box.	
9. Ring the lunch bell, grab a sandwich and dash to the class.	
10. Sing a quick song and munch lunch.	

Decodable sentences: Oxford Level 3, Yellow Book Band

	✓
1. Ben might bring a hat and coat too.	
2. Look at the moonlight on the path in the rain.	
3. Grab some toast and look at the book with me.	
4. Three freezing kings in a green boat. Splish! Splash!	
5. Magnus will now sort the rubbish and go to his shed.	
6. Fork the soil in the garden and plant the turnip seeds.	
7. Slink is on the prowl looking for a sandwich.	
8. Do not disturb Magnus and Turnip for now.	
9. The car is at the top of the main car park.	
10. Pip took a brown liquid, a silver powder and a cork. Pow!	

Silly sentences

Teacher notes

Photocopy the charts (enlarge if possible) and ask children to read the sentences across each row.
Then model selecting one word from each column to make an entirely new sentence.

Oxford Level 1+, Pink Book Band

1	Ben	in	a	pot.
2	Pip	on		pit.
3	Jin	is	the	cat.
4	Slink	got		dog.

Oxford Level 2, Red Book Band

1	He	got	the	snack.
2	She	lifts		shed.
3	We	has	a	chicken.
4	Magnus	rang		drink.
5	Mr Trainer	hid	that	fish.

Oxford Level 3, Yellow Book Band

1	Miss Linen	brings	the	cloth.
2	Magnus	was	a	farmer.
3	Turnip	is	my	pet.
4	Mrs Butterworth	has	that	popcorn.
5	Mrs Molten	took	this	powder.

Response cards

Teacher notes

Photocopy the cards; laminate them and cut them up. Make into sets using a tag or clip for children to use.

I'm listening …	I have something to say …
I agree with that!	I have a question …
I don't agree.	This makes me think of …
I'm not sure …	

Reading partners

Before reading

1. Find a place to sit together and make sure you can both see the book.

2. Make sure the reader holds the book and turns the pages.

During reading

1. The reader reads aloud in a clear voice.

2. The listener shows they are listening.

After reading

1. Talk about the story or the information.

2. Reread a page or two together.

Feedback on reading

Feedback is information given to the learner and/or the teacher about the learner's performance relative to learning goals. It should aim towards (and be capable of producing) improvement in students' learning.[1]

Providing effective feedback is challenging. Research suggests that it should be specific, accurate and clear... and provide specific guidance on how to improve.[2]

In Reception/Primary 1, feedback to children follows on logically from observation during adult-supported and child-initiated activities and will be mainly spoken and immediate. It is a two-way process—adult to child and child to adult—and serves three main purposes:

1. It helps the learner to know what they have done well and give next learning steps.
2. It helps the adult identify next steps in learning, adjusting provision as necessary.
3. It supports learners participating actively with the learning process.

Here are some points to consider when eliciting and giving feedback in Reception/Primary 1.

- Create a learning environment where children's responses and comments are welcomed and positively responded to.
- When engaging in talk activities, ensure there is a balance of adult and child talk; give just enough thinking time to allow the child to respond but interject to keep the talk focused.
- Make it part of a learning conversation or dialogue; listen to children's responses.
- Be specific and clear in your praise – avoid generic comments such as "well done" or "that was good reading". A beginner reader needs to know what they have done well, so, for example, say: "I liked the way you used your sounds to blend that unknown word."
- Feed back on children's attitudes and efforts as well as reading, e.g. perseverance, self-checking, asking for help.
- Use closed questions sparingly; remember that children need thinking time to answer a question so pause for this; encourage the children to ask questions too.
- Model 'thinking aloud' for the children; use tentative language to demonstrate how it is good to ask questions and to sometimes feel unsure.

---

[1] Higgins, S., Katsipataki, M., Kokotsaki, D., Coleman, R., Major, L.E., & Coe, R., 2014. *The Sutton Trust - Education Endowment Foundation Teaching and Learning Toolkit*, London: Education Endowment Foundation.

[2] Ibid

The *Reading journey record* photocopiable master (page 24) can be used as a prompt to initiate a learning conversation about reading and can also serve as a record to return to with the child as they develop as a reader.

Certificates, stickers and rewards can be motivating and, as mentioned above, these should be for specific skills or attitudes: see the *Ask me!* photocopiable master (page 37). They encourage children to talk about their reading, can serve as a prompt for parents and carers and also support a cumulative record of feedback if copies are kept in a learning journey folder or simple wallet.

Celebrate reading and share the success

It is key that, right from the outset, children feel they are 'on the road' to reading. Acknowledging specific small steps of reading progress, including positive attitudes to reading, will provide those all-important incentives for pupils. A simple reward system can act as a way of quickly feeding back to children, efficiently recording observations for staff and for informing parents and carers. Rewards can be stored in a simple individual folder or card, kept centrally and then taken home periodically. See the *Reading heroes* photocopiable master (page 38).

Ask me!

Teacher notes

Photocopy the templates below on to paper or card. Fill them in for children where appropriate.

HERO ACADEMY

Name: ....

I've been learning new words.

....

....

....

Ask me about them!

Date:

HERO ACADEMY

Name: ....

I'm reading Hero Academy books.
Let's talk about

....

Date:

HERO ACADEMY

Name: ....

I'm moving on in my reading journey.

Ask me why!

Date:

HERO ACADEMY

Name: ....

I've been reading

....

Ask me about

....

Date:

Reading heroes

Teacher notes

Photocopy the templates below on to paper or card. Fill them in for children where appropriate.

Name: ....

Slink thinks I'm a reading hero today because …

....

Date:

Name: ....

I'm a reading hero!
Ask me why!

Date:

Name: ....

Super reader award

Ask me why!

Date:

Name: ....

I can read the following words:

....

....

....

Date:

Engaging parents and carers

There is much evidence of the positive impact of parent and carer support on a child's early school experience. This is particularly so for their literacy development in Reception/Primary 1 and beyond; the benefits of parents reading aloud to children, sharing books with them from an early age and, importantly, of continuing to read to and with children when they can read, are the subject of many studies both in the UK and abroad. A number of studies have also flagged the positive effect of encouraging parents to talk to and with their children about their learning. This is, of course, an important factor in developing reading comprehension and expanding a child's vocabulary – both vital contributors to becoming a successful and motivated reader.

In the *Review of best practice in parental engagement* (DfE 2011), researchers identified effective practice in schools' engagement of parents and carers. Key to this was devising a whole-school strategy to engage parents in children's learning and providing clear guidance for parents on specific aspects of learning and how to use this information with their child.

> *Effort focused on some aspects of literacy – for example, training parents to teach specific reading skills to their children – is more likely to be effective than effort focused on other aspects – for example, encouraging parents to listen to their children to read.*[1]

Points for consideration in engaging parents and carers with their child's reading

In your school, consider how you offer:

- guidance to parents and carers about how early reading can be supported at home,
- advice on specific aspects of learning to read, e.g. the phonics skill of blending, paying attention to punctuation,
- further and ongoing support for parents of children who can read, e.g. to improve reading fluency, to support higher-order reading skills such as inference, or to acquire a life-long interest in books and reading.

---

[1] Goodall, J., and Vorhaus, J., with the help of Carpentieri, JD., Brooks, G., Akerman, R., and Harris, A., 2011. *Review of best practice in parental engagement*, Department for Education.

Here are some suggestions for activities to inform parents about reading and how they can support their child in the early stages of learning to read.

- Invite new parents and carers to a meeting about the 'what and how' of the teaching of reading in school.

- Provide workshops and/or 'drop-ins' about specific aspects of learning to read, e.g. phonics; ensure there is clear guidance on how this can be used at home.

- Invite parents and carers to observe a class phonics session or shared or guided reading session in school, or do a phonics or guided reading session with a group of parents.

- Emphasize the wide variety of reading tasks and the importance of adults at home acting as reading 'role models'.

- Have an ongoing and changing display of all reading done in school and home by all adults and children, e.g. a meals supervisor reading a menu in the dining hall, the admin officer reading a report, a parent reading a DIY manual, a grandparent reading a newspaper.

- Provide a simple booklet of rhymes (this could be done online), poems and songs that the children are learning in class or in assemblies that can be used at home.

- Encourage joining the local library; where appropriate, ask a local librarian to come into school and set up an informal 'join here' stall; stress the importance of learning to 'browse' books.

- Loan *story sacks* or *book bags* (books to read together with suggested play activities to do at home); parents and carers could be involved in the creation of these as a central resource.

- Periodically provide lists of quality children's books—both classics and new books—to encourage wider reading; these could be on display in a communal or library area of the school so parents see it.

- Provide details of useful technology, apps and websites—such as Oxford Owl—where parents and carers can access further advice, e-books and activities for supporting their child at home.

Oxford Owl is an award-winning website supporting children's learning at school and at home. *Oxford Owl for Home* is a dedicated parent website that provides advice for parents and carers to support their children through primary school. It helps parents and carers to approach learning with confidence and enthusiasm, including ideas for everyday learning activities, phonics help and videos of professional storytellers.

Oxford OWL

Clear guidance about specific aspects of reading is key for parents and carers; they need to know what they should do and why it helps their child with reading. It should be made clear that they are *supporting* the teaching of reading. Below are some suggestions for workshops that could be provided.

- Phonics: particularly articulation of the phonemes and blending 'all through the word' skills. You could do this within the context of introducing them to the **Hero Academy** books.

- The importance of adult and child book talk: talk before and after reading to aid comprehension; using questions sparingly!

- The importance of understanding vocabulary: making the vocabulary used in texts part of children's own vocabulary.

- The importance of not correcting too soon: giving children time to sort out any difficulties and develop resilience when facing a challenge; 'prompting and praising' – the acknowledgement of good effort and attitudes, e.g. "I liked the way you got a bit muddled but then you went back and blended that word again. Well done."

The **Hero Academy** books each have inside cover notes that offer a structure and prompts for parents and carers reading with a child at home. Provide parents with a short introduction to the **Hero Academy** series to inform their book talk discussions with the child. See *An introduction to Hero Academy for parents and carers* photocopiable master (on the following page). The reading tips grid can be photocopied or adapted and made available to parents and carers as bookmarks that can be used as a prompt when reading with their child.

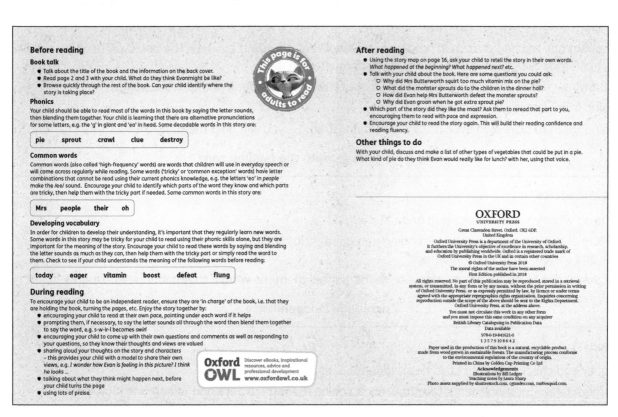

OXFORD
UNIVERSITY PRESS

Great Clarendon Street, Oxford, OX2 6DP,
United Kingdom

Oxford University Press is a department of the University of Oxford.
It furthers the University's objective of excellence in research, scholarship,
and education by publishing worldwide. Oxford is a registered trade mark of
Oxford University Press in the UK and in certain other countries

© Oxford University Press 2018
The moral rights of the author have been asserted
First Edition published in 2018

All rights reserved. No part of this publication may be reproduced, stored in a retrieval
system, or transmitted, in any form or by any means, without the prior permission in writing
of Oxford University Press, or as expressly permitted by law, by licence or under terms
agreed with the appropriate reprographics rights organization. Enquiries concerning
reproduction outside the scope of the above should be sent to the Rights Department,
Oxford University Press, at the address above.

You must not circulate this work in any other form
and you must impose this same condition on any acquirer

British Library Cataloguing in Publication Data
Data available

978-0-19-841621-0
1 3 5 7 9 10 8 6 4 2

Paper used in the production of this book is a natural, recyclable product
made from wood grown in sustainable forests. The manufacturing process conforms
to the environmental regulations of the country of origin.
Printed in China by Golden Cup Printing Co Ltd
Acknowledgements
Illustrations by Bill Ledger
Teaching notes by Laura Sharp
Photo assets supplied by shutterstock.com, cgtrader.com, turbosquid.com.

An introduction to Hero Academy for parents and carers

Welcome to Hero Academy!

Hero Academy is a series of highly motivating books set around a school for superheroes!

Like every school, the heroes have lessons, make friends, play and explore. In order to remain anonymous, they have superhero costumes and have alternative superhero names. Together they work as a team to defeat villains and protect the academy and Lexis City.

All the stories support the phonics teaching that your child will be experiencing in class. For more support with phonics, ask at your school or visit Oxford Owl: **www.oxfordowl.co.uk**

Oxford OWL

Reading with your child at home

Before you begin

- Make time to read together every day for short focused sessions – 10 minutes is fine! This develops the reading 'habit' and makes it part of your child's routine.
- Make sure there are no distractions, such as the TV, radio, tablets, mobiles etc, so you and your child can give your undivided attention to reading.

Make reading an enjoyable and stress-free habit

Get ready to read

- Talk about any reading your child has done in school that day. Do they know the book you're about to read? What can they tell you about the story or the characters in it?
- Ensure your child is in charge of the book, i.e. that they hold the book and turn the pages!
- Remind them to read in a clear voice.
- Remind them to have a go even if they are finding it hard – you will help them.

Help your child get into the reading zone

Prompt and praise

- Focus on what your child does well and tell them.
- Use lots of specific praise for good reading and good attitudes, e.g. "You got muddled there, but you went back and sorted it out. Great reading!"
- Give them time to have a go at unfamiliar words, but tell them the word if they continue to struggle.

Encourage independence

Talk about it

- Go back and check that your child has understood any unfamiliar words.
- Ask them a few questions about the story, encouraging them to go back and reread a section where necessary.
- Can they retell the events in order?
- Talk about the story, e.g. why did the character do that?
- Give them time to express their thoughts, views and opinions.

Understanding what has been read is important

If, for any reason, your child is reluctant to read then don't abandon the session completely. Read to them instead (or take it in turns to read a page), and talk about the book so that there is still a regular reading session.

Phonic and vocabulary overview for Reception/Primary 1

The **Hero Academy** stories follow a fine phonic progression in line with *Letters and Sounds*. A specific breakdown of the phonic words used in each book is given on the following pages.

Oxford Level	Book Band		Book no.*	Book title	*Letters and Sounds* Phase	Grapheme Phoneme Correspondences (GPCs)	Common words (HFWs: decodable)	Common exception words (HFWs: tricky)	Suffixes and endings	Contractions
1	Lilac	A	1	Cat Chase	Phase 1	Wordless	n/a	n/a	n/a	None before Year 1
			2	Jin Can Fly						
		B	3	The Lost Cat	Phase 2, Set 1	s, a, t, p	n/a	n/a	n/a	
			4	Jin's First Day						
1+	Pink	A	5	Pip's Prank	Phase 2, Set 2	m, i, n, d	in, is, it, and, a	n/a	-s	
			6	It is a Tip!						
		B	7	Cat in a Cap	Phase 2, Set 3	g, o, c, k	on, can, got, not	n/a		
			8	Stop, Cat!						
		C	9	Tuck In	Phase 2, Set 4	ck, e, u, r	get, up	to, the		
			10	Magnus is Stuck						
		D	11	Jin is Ill	Phase 2, Set 5	h, b, f, l, ff, ll, ss	of, off, back, big	no, go, I		
			12	Ben Helps						
2	Red	A	13	Jin Lifts Off	Phase 3, Set 6	j, v, w, x	will	n/a		
			14	Will the Reds Win?						
		B	15	The Zipbot	Phase 3, Set 7	y, z, zz, qu	n/a	he, she	-es	
			16	Pip's Mess						
		C	17	Slink's Snack	Phase 3	ch, sh, th, ng, nk	that, this, then, them, with	me, we, be		
			18	Fix That Bell!						
3	Yellow	A	19	It is Freezing		ai, ee, igh, oa	see, too	was, her	-ing	
			20	Win the Cup!						
		B	21	Turnip is Missing	Phase 3	oo (look), oo (zoom), ar, or, ur	look, for	my, you		
			22	Zoom Food						
		C	23	Stuck in the Storm		ow, oi, ear, ure, air, er	down, now	they, all, are	-er	
			24	The Fizzing Mixture						

*Book numbers

Book numbers are given here for teacher reference only to reflect the small steps of progression in the **Hero Academy** series. The books themselves are not numbered and can be read in any order (depending on the level the pupil is reading at).

Oxford Level 1/1+, Lilac/Pink Book Bands

Book no.	Book title	Letters and Sounds Phase	Words with Phonic Phase GPCs		Common words (HFWs: decodable)	Common exception words (HFWs: tricky)	Developing vocabulary*	Suffixes and endings
1	Cat Chase	Phase 1	Wordless		n/a	n/a	Talk only: woman, worried, panicked, skidding, grass	n/a
2	Jin Can Fly		Wordless		n/a	n/a	Talk only: Jin, determined, hovering, air	n/a
3	The Lost Cat	Phase 2, Set 1	a	tap (p2), pat (p7, p11)	n/a	n/a	Talk only: Pip, crouching, down, car	n/a
			t					
			p					
4	Jin's First Day		s	tap (p2, p5, p6, p9), sssss (p4, p7), pat (p8, p10)	n/a	n/a	Talk only: Jin, amazed, sight, academy	n/a
			a					
			t					
			p					
5	Pip's Prank	Phase 2, Set 2	m	mad (p9)	it (p4), in (p4), is (p9), and (p11)	n/a	Ben (p2, p4, p9, p11), Slink (p2), prank (p1)	-s: tips (p4)
			i	Pip (p2, p11), pit (p3), tips (p4), it (p4), in (p4), is (p9), sit (p11)				
			d	mad (p9), and (p11)				
			n	in (p4), and (p11)				
6	It is a Tip!		m	mad (p4), mat (p6)	it (p3, p10), is (p3, p4, p6), and (p11), a (p3)	n/a	Ben (p2), Mrs Molten (p2, p4), Magnus (p2), Slink (p2), tip (p3, p10), pan (p8, p9)	n/a
			i	Pip (p2, p6), it (p3, p10), is (p3, p4, p6), tip (p3, p10), tin (p9), sit (p11), sip (p11)				
			d	mad (p4), sad (p6), and (p11)				
			n	pan (p8, p9), tin (p9), and (p11)				

*Developing vocabulary

In these charts and on the inside covers of each book, we've identified some challenging words and (occasionally) phrases readers will encounter. These 'challenge words' are important for the meaning of the story and to develop children's comprehension skills by broadening their vocabulary. Children will be capable of using their phonics knowledge to read these words. Challenge words include some conceptually challenging words (e.g. words with dual meanings, such as 'tip'), simple compound words, simple two-syllable words and words with adjacent consonants. The only truly 'non decodable' words in these stories are the occasional character name, e.g. Mrs Butterworth. However these names are frequently repeated and quickly become familiar (similar to common exception words) so we have included them in these stories.

Oxford Level 1+, Pink Book Band cont.

Book no.	Book title	Letters and Sounds Phase	Words with Phonic Phase GPCs		Common words (HFWs: decodable)	Common exception words (HFWs: tricky)	Developing vocabulary	Suffixes and endings
7	Cat in a Cap	Phase 2, Set 3	g	got (p3, p11), gap (p7)	can (p2, p8), not (p5), got (p3, p11), on (p5)	n/a	Slink (p2, p4, p6, p7, p11), pom-poms (p4, p5, p10), gap (p7), skids (p7)	-s: pom-poms (p4, p5, p10), spots (p4), skids (p7)
			o	got (p3, p11), pom-poms (p4, p5, p10), spots (p4), not (p5), on (p5), cod (p11)				
			c	can (p2, p8), cap (p4, p9), cat (p5, p10), cod (p11)				
			k	kit (p3), skids (p7)				
8	Stop, Cat!		g	gas (p4), gasp (p8), got (p10)	can (p2, p3), not (p3), got (p10)	n/a	Jin (p2), Slink (p2, p4), nap (p3), gasp (p8), kit (p11)	-s: taps (p11)
			o	not (p3), cod (p4), top (p6), stop (p8), got (p10), pop (p11)				
			c	can (p2, p3), cat (p3, p6, p8), cod (p4)				
			k	kit (p11)				
9	Tuck In	Phase 2, Set 4	ck	kick (p2), tuck (p3, p11), picks (p4, p10)	get (p7), up (p4, p10)	to (p7), the (p4, p5, p7, p10)	Slink (p2, p3, p5), Magnus (p2, p10), tuck in (p3, p11), skids (p8)	-s: gets (p3, p11), picks (p4, p10), runs (p5, p7), spots (p5), spins (p6), skids (p8)
			e	gets (p3, p11), get (p7), pet (p10				
			u	tuck (p3, p11), up (p4, p10), runs (p5, p7)				
			r	rat (p4, p5, p10), runs (p5, p7)				
10	Magnus is Stuck		ck	pick (p2), rocks (p2), picks (p4, p5), sack (p4), stuck (p7), rock (p8, p9)	get (p8), up (p2, p4, p5)	to (p8), the (p9)	Magnus (p2, p4, p5, p7, p11), sack (p4), gust (p5)	-s: rocks (p2), picks (p4, p5), runs (p8), gets (p9, p11), spins (p10)
			e	g get (p8), gets (p9, p11)				
			u	up (p2, p4, p5), gust (p5), stuck (p7), runs (p8)				
			r	rocks (p2), runs (p8), rock (p8, p9)				
11	Jin is Ill	Phase 2, Set 5	h	hot (p3, p7, p8, p10), hop (p4)	of (p7), off (p5), back (p7), big (p7)	no (p4), go (p2, p7), I (p3, p8, p9, p10)	Mrs Butterworth (p2), Jin (p2, p3, p6, p7, p11), bug (illness) (p3), lemon (p7)	-s: gets (p7)
			b	Ben (p2, p10), bad (p3, p6), bug (p3), bed (p4, p7), back (p7), big (p7)				
			f	fan (p4), fuss (p4), fun (p11)				
			l	luck (p6), lemon (p7)				
			ff	off (p5)				
			ll	ill (p3, p10), well (p6)				
			ss	fuss (p4)				
12	Ben Helps		h	help (p3, p5, p9, p11), helps (p4), huff (p4), has (p5), hits (p7)	of (p5), off (p8), big (p10)	no (p8), go (p11), I (p3, p5, p9, p11)	Miss Baker (p2, p8), Slink (p2, p8), mess (p10), fast (p2, p11)	-s: helps (p4), gets (p6), hits (p7), drops (p7), tells (p8), mops (p10)
			b	Ben (p2, p4, p6, p7, p10, p11), bin (p7), bad (p8), big (p10)				
			f	fast (p2, p11), fun (p10)				
			l	help (p3, p5, p9, p11), helps (p4)				
			ff	huff (p4), puff (p4), off (p8)				
			ll	tells (p8)				
			ss	Miss (p2, p5, p8), mess (p10)				

Oxford Level 2, Red Book Band

Book no.	Book title	*Letters and Sounds* Phase	Words with Phonic Phase GPCs		Common words (HFWs: decodable)	Common exception words (HFWs: tricky)	Developing vocabulary	Suffixes and endings
13	Jin Lifts Off		j	Jin (p2, p3, p4, p6, p7, p11, p12, p13, p14), just (p13)	will (p3)	n/a	Mr Trainer (p2), Slink (p2), pass (p3, p12), ducks (p6), dips (p6), twists (p7), spins (p8)	-s: ducks (p6), dips (p6), twists (p7), spins (p8), lands (p11), seconds (p13)
			v	vet (p9), seven (p13)				
			w	will (p3), twists (p7), well (p13)				
			x	next (p8), six (p8), box (p10, p11)				
14	Will the Reds Win?	Phase 3, Set 6	j	Jin (p2, p3, p8, p9, p13, p14), jogs (p7), jets (p13)	will (p10, p12)	n/a	fast (p5), jets (p13)	-s: gets (p3, p5, p7, p14), vests (p4, p10), hits (p4), runs (p5, p7), bats (p6, p8), jogs (p7), jets (p13), reds (p15)
			v	vest (p3), vests (p4, p10), seven (p5)				
			w	will (p10, p12), win (p15)				
			x	next (p6, p8, p10), six (p7)				
15	The Zipbot		y	yet (p4), yes (p4)	n/a	he (p13), she (p5)	zigzags (p6), grass (p6), skids (p6)	-s: sits (p5), taps (p5, p10), zigzags (p6), hits (p7), spins (p8), skids (p8), runs (p12), stops (p14)
			z	Zipbot (p3, p5, p6, p8, p9, p10, p14), zigzags (p6)				
			zz	buzz (p5, p6)				
		Phase 3, Set 7	qu	quack (p10), quick (p11, p13)				
16	Pip's Mess		y	yuck (p3), yells (p10)	n/a	he (p14), she (p5)	Mrs Molten (p2), Slink (p2, p8, p12, p14), fizzes (p6)	-es: fizzes (p6)
			z	zap (p11), zip (p12)				
			zz	buzz (p3, p4, p7, p15), fizzes (p6)				
			qu	liquid (p4, p5, p6, p8, p10, p11), quick (p10)				
17	Slink's Snack		ch	checks (p5), chicken (p8), chips (p9, p14), lunch (p13), such (p14)	that (p13), this (p11), then (p9, p12)	me (p11)	Miss Baker (p2), peckish (p3), mash (p9, p14)	n/a
			sh	peckish (p3), fresh (p4), fish (p4, p7), dish (p9), mash (p9, p14), shock (p12), crash (p13)				
			th	then (p9, p12), this (p11), that (p13), bath (p15)				
			ng	clang (p13), long (p15)				
			nk	Slink (p2, p5, p7, p8, p10, p12, p13, p14, p15), drink (p10), sink (p15)				
18	Fix That Bell!	Phase 3	ch	lunch (p3, p6, p14), chips (p5), much (p7), sandwich (p15)	that (p9), this (p7), then (p6, p14), them (p12), with (p5)	we (p4, p9), me (p9), be (p6, p9)	Mrs Butterworth (p2), peckish (p4), dash (p4), pass (p9), pulls (p10), springs (metal coils) (p11, p12)	-es: rushes (p12), fixes (p13)
			sh	peckish (p4), dash (p4), fish (p5), rushes (p12)				
			th	with (p5), then (p6, p14), this (p7), think (p7), that (p9), them (p12), thanks (p15)				
			ng	rings (p3, p6, p7, p14), ring (p3, p6, p7, p10, p14), ping (p11), springs (p11, p12)				
			nk	drink (p5, p15), think (p7), thanks (p15)				

Oxford Level 3, Yellow Book Band

Book no.	Book title	Letters and Sounds Phase	Words with Phonic Phase GPCs		Common words (HFWs: decodable)	Common exception words (HFWs: tricky)	Developing vocabulary	Suffixes and endings
19	It is Freezing	Phase 3	ai	wait (p3), trail (p5), tail (p12)	see (p14), too (p6, p13)	her (p3)	fast (p5), push (p6, p7), groans (p6)	n/a
			ee	freezing (p3), needs (p3, p12, p13), three (p10), see (p14)				
			igh	sighs (p8), light (p8), high (p9)				
			oa	coat (p3), loads (p4), groans (p6), coal (p10), cloak (p13)				
20	Win the Cup!		ai	tail (p13), complain (p14), train (p15)	see (p5), too (p5, p7)	was (p14), her (p9)	boasts (p4, p6, p8), fast (p5), complain (p14)	n/a
			ee	see (p5), feet (p5, p12), need (p10, p15), keep (p10), agree (p10)				
			igh	high (p7), might (p10)				
			oa	boasts (p4, p6, p8), floats (p7)				
21	Turnip is Missing		oo (look)	looking (p3), book (p3), look (p4), looks (p5)	look (p4), for (p4, p5, p9)	my (p3), you (p4, p12)	fast (p2), darts (p4), scoots (p7), scoops (p11)	-ing: looking (p3), missing (p3)
			oo (zoom)	room (p4), scoots (p7), soon (p10), food (p10), scoops (p11)				
			ar	darts (p4), garden (p6)				
			or	for (p4, p5, p9), thorns (p8, p13), sweetcorn (p9)				
			ur	Turnip (p2, p3, p4, p5, p6, p7, p8, p9, p10, p11, p12, p14, p15), bursts (p3), Turnip's (p13), fur (p13)				
22	Zoom Food	Phase 3	oo (look)	look (p5), cook (p5), books (p5), book (p6), looks (p6), good (p6, p15)	look (p5), for (p8)	my (p5), you (p10)	Mrs Butterworth (p2, p7), zoom (p2, p3, p8, p10, p11), fast (p3, p4, p8, p12), beetroot (p7), burst of speed (p8), past (p11), pull (p14)	-ing: going (p12)
			oo (zoom)	zoom (p2, p3, p8, p10, p11), food (p4, p8, p10), beetroot (p7), spoons (p8), zooms (p10, p11, p13), too (p10, p12), shoots (p12)				
			ar	stars (p12)				
			or	popcorn (p7), for (p8)				
			ur	turnip (p7), burst (p8), slurps (p8), turn (p12), turns (p13)				
23	Stuck in the Storm		ow	power (p2), meow (p4), frowns (p4), now (p5), down (p8), towels (p15)	down (p8), now (p5)	they (p6, p8), all (p7), are (p3, p8)	thunder (p4), avoid (p5), fast (p6), skid (p11), skidding (p12), appears (p13), soaking (p14)	-ing: soaking (p14)
			oi	avoid (p5), soil (p11)				
			ear	hear (p4), clear (p9, p12), appears (p13)				
			ure	sure (p9)				
			air	air (p4), hair (p14)				
			er	power (p2), thunder (p4), her (p11, p12), better (p15)				
24	The Fizzing Mixture	Phase 3	ow	powders (p3), powder (p4, p5), frowns (p5), how (p9, p12), down (p9, p10, p14), now (p11)	down (p9, p10, p14), now (p11)	they (p3, p11), all (p5), are (p9)	Mrs Molten (p2, p3, p6, p7, p12, p14, p15), fast (p2), mixture (p4, p5, p6), frowns (p5), splashes (p6), darts up (p13), pass (p15)	-ing: going (p9) -er: darker (p5)
			oi	spoil (p5), boils (p6)				
			ear	clear (p5), dear (p7), near (p8)				
			ure	sure (p4), mixture (p4, p5, p6), cure (p12, p13)				
			air	air (p7), stairs (p10)				
			er	powders (p3), powder (p4, p5), darker (p5), her (p9), ladder (p11, p14)				

Progression with Oxford Levels at Reception/Primary 1

The **Hero Academy** books are finely-levelled using rigorous criteria. These criteria pay close attention to the structural features of a text, such as sentence complexity, and also look at factors which enhance children's enjoyment of books, such as character and plot progression. In this way, as well as developing reading skills and stamina, children also develop a real enthusiasm for books.

Oxford Level 1

What texts are like:

- books may be wordless,
- there are opportunities to learn about directionality of print, book orientation, etc.,
- texts support Phase 1 of *Letters and Sounds* and introduce early Phase 2 grapheme-phoneme correspondences,
- there is a simple, gradual building-up of words,
- text may not be in whole sentences,
- features such as labels, speech bubbles, sound effects and environmental print may be included,
- pictures support the story and enable children to practise retelling,
- the stories relate to children's experiences – even in a school for heroes!

Oxford Level 1,
Lilac Book Band:
The Lost Cat

Oxford Level 1,
Lilac Book Band:
Jin's First Day

Oxford Level 1+

What texts are like:

- stories have a very clear beginning, middle and end,
- text is aligned to Phase 2 of *Letters and Sounds*,
- there are opportunities to practise common and common exception/irregular words (high-frequency and 'tricky' words),
- reading is supported by predictable and repeated words, phrases and sentences,
- language structures are simple and mimic natural speech patterns,
- text allows children to pose and answer basic questions, e.g. *Why did Pip pick up the rock?*
- there are opportunities to begin to exercise simple judgements (likes and dislikes),
- features such as labels, speech bubbles, sound effects and environmental print are included,
- the stories relate to children's experiences – even in a school for heroes!

Pip can tip it.

A cap.

Oxford Level 1+,
Pink Book Band:
Cat in a Cap

Oxford Level 1+,
Pink Book Band:
Magnus is Stuck

Magnus picks up a sack.

A gust picks up Magnus!

Oxford Level 2

What texts are like:

- stories have a very clear beginning, middle and end,
- text is aligned to Phase 3 of *Letters and Sounds*, with opportunities to practise digraphs,
- there are further opportunities to practise common and common exception/irregular words (high-frequency and 'tricky' words),
- reading is supported by predictable and repeated words, phrases and sentences,
- language structures are simple and mimic natural speech patterns and use familiar vocabulary,
- text allows children to pose and answer basic questions, e.g. *Why did Slink want a snack?*
- features such as labels, speech bubbles, sound effects and environmental print are included.

 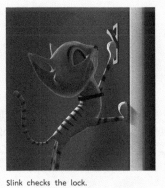

Oxford Level 2,
Red Book Band:
Slink's Snack

Oxford Level 2,
Red Book Band:
The Zipbot

Oxford Level 3

What texts are like:

- stories have a very clear beginning, middle and end,
- text is aligned to Phase 3 of *Letters and Sounds*, with opportunities to practise digraphs and trigraphs,
- there are further opportunities to practise common and common exception/irregular words (high-frequency and 'tricky' words),
- reading is supported by predictable and repeated words, phrases and sentences,
- language structures are simple and mimic natural speech patterns and use familiar vocabulary,
- children begin to deepen their responses to the text,
- there are opportunities to practise basic inference,
- features such as labels, speech bubbles, sound effects and environmental print are included.

Oxford Level 3,
Yellow Book Band:
The Fizzing Mixture

Oxford Level 3,
Yellow Book Band:
It is Freezing

Guided reading support

It will take time for children to become familiar with the routine, but early exposure to guided reading sessions is essential to give children maximum opportunities to practise and apply new learning in relation to both word reading and comprehension skills.

On the following pages, you will find detailed session plans for running guided reading sessions using each of the books in the **Hero Academy** series at Reception/Primary 1. During the sessions, it is important that the teacher/teaching assistant shares their thoughts (as an expert reader) aloud using phrases such as "I wonder why...", "I'm puzzled by...", "I think that...", "I like the way..." before asking the group the suggested question prompts in the session plans. 'Thinking aloud' will help developing readers understand the thought processes that are implicit before, during and after reading. It will also invite discussion and encourage the group to share their thoughts, building on or opposing the thoughts of others. The guidance below provides further clarification about the facilitator's role during these sessions.

Recommended teaching sequence

Before reading

It is important that children become 'hooked' into the new story to ensure that they are engaged and enthused from the outset. This will involve the teacher/teaching assistant prompting children to activate their prior knowledge, make predictions and make connections with their personal experiences. Previewing the text to familiarize the children with the front cover, title, blurb, text type (where appropriate), and a brief scan through the text before children begin to read independently, is useful (especially where the children might be faced with unfamiliar text features or a new layout). It will also encourage them to make predictions and explore any unfamiliar vocabulary before they begin to read on their own. The session plans provide guidance on different reading strategies during this part of the sequence. The aim is for you to model and review an identified reading strategy that the children have previously been taught and set high expectations for them to use this strategy during reading. For example, using their grapheme-phoneme correspondence knowledge in order to blend to read unfamiliar words, reading with expression, or a comprehension-based strategy such as using the *Feelings fan* photocopiable master (PCM 28) to help them explore and empathize with the feelings of characters in the story.

> **Additional support:** A number of additional resources have been included as photocopiable masters (PCMs 25–31) to use as visual prompts to further support children's engagement and independence in the sessions. Full guidance on when and how to use these is provided in the individual session notes. A number of the tools are used in more than one session so you might find it useful to laminate each tool so that they can be used on multiply occasions. Storing these in individual plastic wallets (one per child) will allow the children to make choices and refer to these tools on other occasions during or after reading.

During reading

It is crucial that children have their own copy of the text so that they can maintain focus and read at their own pace. Children may initially find this difficult – especially if they have no previous experience of reading independently in a small group context. A number of strategies might prove useful in supporting children to concentrate and build their attention span. Inviting each child to read to a soft toy, using one of the *Superhero bookmarks* (page 17) as a point for them to read up to before pausing for discussion, or giving them a timer and asking them to read until the timer runs out, will all build children's confidence in reading independently. During reading, you will have the opportunity to tune into individuals to check their understanding and encourage problem-solving. The detailed session notes suggest places to pause in the story to discuss what is happening and elicit thinking, using phrases such as "I wonder why…" Keep a balance between stopping to ensure children have understood what is happening and keeping the flow of the story moving. As children become more confident at applying the relevant reading strategies independently, you can reduce the number of pauses. This is reflected in the gaps between pauses which increase progressively as they move through the Oxford Levels/Book Bands. You might find it useful to jot down relevant assessment points on the *Phonics skills and knowledge progress check* charts (pages 105-107) or the *Comprehension skills and behaviours* checklist (page 108). Make time to provide specific 'in the moment feedback' as children apply appropriate reading strategies, as this will help them to understand their own reading progress; building their resilience, self-regulation and metacognition. For example, "I liked the way you looked carefully at the GPCs in this word before blending them. That's a good strategy to help you read an unfamiliar word. Well done." Further guidance is given in the *Feedback in Reading* section of this handbook.

After reading

There are two elements to this part of the sequence; the first is to briefly return to the text to check if there are any words that the children found difficult to decode/ understand alongside clarifying any misconceptions that have arisen. (It is useful to give the children sticky notes to use during the session to note down any words that caused difficulties and have not already been addressed individually during reading. This prevents children from stalling or becoming distracted if the adult is tuned into a different child at that point). The second element is to involve the children in a 'book talk' discussion inviting children to share their thinking, respond to and build on the ideas put forward by other members of the group. Specific prompts are suggested in the session notes along with activities that will involve the children in exploring the plot, characters or themes in more detail. Don't feel constrained by the suggested prompts – have the confidence to make a judgement and go with the children's lines of enquiry rather than adhere too rigidly to the script. The *Ask me!* labels (page 37) can be used to encourage children to talk about their reading with a wider audience (giving them further opportunities to revisit and recall what they have read), whilst the *Reading heroes* badges (page 38) can be used to celebrate and share children's progress with colleagues and parents/carers.

Other things to do

The speaking and listening/writing activities provide further opportunities for children to deepen their understanding of the stories they have read and use familiar language and structures from their reading as part of their own dialogues and writing. They also provide further opportunities for the children to reread each story to develop fluency and stamina. In addition, the session plans include a wide variety of activities linked both to the topics and ideas addressed in these stories and to other areas of the curriculum to help children make connections in their learning.

Cat Chase

Story summary

In this wordless story, a boy called Ben notices a runaway dog chasing a cat (Slink). He uses his super-speed to catch the dog and return it to its owner.

Additional resources: Photocopiable master (PCM) 1: Order the story: *Cat Chase*; PCM 25: Speech bubble.

Phonics and vocabulary checker*

Phonics	
Focus GPCs	n/a
Decodable words	n/a
Common words	n/a
Common exception/irregular words ('tricky' words)	n/a

Developing vocabulary
woman, worried, panicked, skidding, grass

The Early Years Foundation Stage Framework**

Early Learning Goals (statutory requirement)		Assessment pointers in this story
ELG 01 Listening and attention	Children listen attentively in a range of situations.	Check children listen carefully to each other's experiences of owning a dog/cat and their predictions of why the cat needs help.
ELG 02 Understanding	Children answer 'how' and 'why' questions about their experiences and in response to stories or events.	Check children understand why Ben had to help catch the dog and why the owner was feeling panicked.
ELG 03 Speaking	Children express themselves effectively, showing awareness of listeners' needs.	Check children can express their ideas about what the dog might be thinking on p4.
ELG 09 Reading	Children demonstrate understanding when talking with others about what they have read.	Check children understand what Ben's superpower is and how he has used it in the story.
		Check children can offer suggestions about what Ben/the dog's owner might be saying on p2, p5, p9 and p10.
		Check children can use the story map on p12 to retell the story.
ELG 10 Writing	Children use their phonic knowledge to write words in ways which match their spoken sounds.	Check whether children have used their knowledge of sounds to attempt to spell some words on their information poster.

Oxford Reading Criterion Scale: Assessment Pre-reading Standard

No.	Criteria	Assessment pointers in this story
1	Can hold books the right way up and turn the pages. (READ)	Check children can hold the book correctly and turn the pages in the right order.
2	Handles books carefully. (READ)	Check children handle the book carefully throughout the reading session.
3	Shows curiosity about books and chooses to look at books independently. (READ)	Check children can show you their favourite part of the story and tell you about it.
14	Can retell an event in a story (may only be brief). (R)	Check children can retell the part of the story where Ben uses his superpower.

---

*For a full phonic breakdown, see the *Phonic and vocabulary overview* section in this handbook.

**Scottish Curriculum for Excellence/Foundation Phase Framework for Wales/Northern Ireland/Cambridge Primary English and International curricula correlation can be found online at: www.oxfordowl.co.uk

Before reading

- Key skills:
  - Look at the illustration on the cover and read the title. Ask children what they think might happen in this story. **(Predicting)**
  - Read the blurb. Ask children who they think Ben is. Why might the cat need Ben's help? **(Predicting)**
  - Ask children if they have a dog or cat and get them to talk about the behaviour of their pets. Share any of your own relevant experience as a model, e.g. *I remember when my dog/cat ...* **(Activating prior knowledge)**
  - Look at Ben's facial expression on the front cover. Ask children what words could they use to talk about how he is feeling. **(Exploring new vocabulary)**

- Strategy check:
  - Remind children that in a wordless book they read the story using the illustrations and their own words. Model using a simple sentence to tell the first part of the story on p2, e.g. *The dog has run away from his owner.* Ask children if they have a different suggestion for p2.

During reading

- Key skills:
  - Help children to look carefully at the illustrations and include as much detail as possible as they read. Praise them for using simple sentences instead of isolated words.
  - Model and encourage children to create sound effects with their voices for the cat/dog. **(Phase 1: General sound discrimination – environmental sounds)**
  - Encourage children to use PCM 25 ('Speech bubble') to express what Ben/the dog's owner might be saying on p2, p5, p9 and p10 as they are reading the story independently. Encourage them to read with expression and change their voice for Ben/the owner. **(Predicting)**
  - Pause on p4. Ask children how Ben could help the cat. **(Inferring)**
  - Pause on p6. Ask children to explain what has happened in the story so far. **(Summarizing)**
  - Ask children to continue reading independently to the end of the story.

After reading

- Return to the text.
- Key skills:
  - Use specific praise to comment on individuals who used the illustrations to help them tell the story.
  - Get children to show you their favourite part of the story and tell you about why they like it. **(Personal response)**
  - Discuss how the dog's owner is feeling. Model a response: *I think the owner feels worried and concerned at the beginning of the story because ...* **(Empathizing)**
  - Return to p4. Discuss what the dog/cat are thinking during the chase. Model a response: *I think the cat is thinking, "Help, this dog wants to eat me for his dinner!"* **(Deducing)**
  - Ask children to think about Ben's superpower. What is it and when/how does he use it in the story? **(Recall and retrieve)**

Other things to do

- Writing activities
  - Use a selection of non-fiction books to find out some new information about cats and dogs. Make a poster. Help children to annotate their poster with labels.
- Speaking, listening and drama
  - Use PCM 1 ('Order the story: *Cat Chase*'). Cut out and order the pictures to retell *Cat Chase* in the correct sequence.
- Cross-curricular links
  - Using modelling clay (or similar), ask children to make the cat or the dog from the story. **(Expressive Arts and Design – exploring media and materials)**

Jin Can Fly

Story summary

This is a wordless story about a boy called Jin. Whilst out for a walk with his family he notices a cat, Slink, is stuck in a tree. Jin uses his superpower to fly up and rescue Slink.

Additional resources: PCM 2: Make a moving picture; PCM 26: Magnifying glass; images of popular superheroes.

Phonics and vocabulary checker*

Phonics	
Focus GPCs	n/a
Decodable words	n/a
Common words	n/a
Common exception/irregular words ('tricky' words)	n/a

Developing vocabulary
Jin, determined, hovering, air

The Early Years Foundation Stage Framework**

Early Learning Goals (statutory requirement)		Assessment pointers in this story
ELG 01 Listening and attention	Children listen to stories, accurately anticipating key events and respond to what they hear with relevant comments, questions or actions.	Check children can predict what might happen next after Jin sees the cat stuck in the tree.
ELG 02 Understanding	Children answer 'how' and 'why' questions about their experiences and in response to stories or events.	Check children understand why the cat climbed the tree and how Jin rescued the cat.
ELG 03 Speaking	Children develop their own narratives and explanations by connecting ideas or events.	Check children can connect ideas to explain how they might try to rescue the cat.
ELG 09 Reading	Children demonstrate understanding when talking with others about what they have read.	Check children can identify how the cat (Slink) is feeling on p10 and why.
ELG 10 Writing	Children use their phonic knowledge to write words in ways which match their spoken sounds.	Check whether children have used their knowledge of sounds to attempt to spell some words in their lists.

Oxford Reading Criterion Scale: Assessment Pre-reading Standard

No.	Criteria	Assessment pointers in this story
1	Can hold books the right way up and turn the pages. (READ)	Check children can hold the book correctly and turn the pages in the right order.
2	Handles books carefully. (READ)	Check children handle the book carefully throughout the reading session.
3	Shows curiosity about books and chooses to look at books independently. (READ)	Check children can return to their favourite part of the story and reread it.
7	Can gain simple meaning from texts using illustrations, when not yet able to read the text itself. (D)	Check children can follow and understand the plot from the images.
14	Can retell an event in a story (may only be brief). (R)	Check children can retell the part of the story when Jin jumps up to rescue the cat. *What happens to Jin?*

---

*For a full phonic breakdown, see the *Phonic and vocabulary overview* section in this handbook.

**Scottish Curriculum for Excellence/Foundation Phase Framework for Wales/Northern Ireland/Cambridge Primary English and International curricula correlation can be found online at: www.oxfordowl.co.uk

Before reading

- Key skills:
  - Share images of popular superheroes that will be familiar to the children including some that can fly. Invite them to tell you about their favourite superhero. **(Activating prior knowledge)**
  - Look at the front cover. Introduce the children to the character Jin. Ask children what they think Jin's superpower might be. Read the title and blurb to confirm this. Ask them why Jin might need to use his superpower during the story. **(Predicting, making connections)**
  - Look at p2. Introduce PCM 26 ('Magnifying glass'), and explain that the magnifying glass will help them to look carefully at the illustrations. Encourage children to look carefully at the image. Jin sees something in the mud. What it is? (Paw prints). Who could the paw prints belong to? Are there any other clues in the picture? **(Exploring vocabulary, previewing the text, inferring)**
- Strategy check:
  - Remind children that in a wordless book they read the story using the illustrations and their own words. Model this using a simple sentence to tell the first part of the story on p2, e.g. *One day Jin goes for a walk in the park with his mum and sister. He spots something in the mud. "Paw prints!" he thinks. "Who might they belong to?"* Ask children if they have a different suggestion for p2.

During reading

- Key skills:
  - Ask children to read on their own to see what animal has made the paw prints. Challenge them to use the magnifying glass to look carefully for clues.
  - Pause on p3. What has Jin spotted in the tree? Give specific 'in the moment' praise: *I like the way you used your magnifying glass to look carefully at the tree in the illustration.* **(Recall and retrieve)**
  - Still on p3: talk about the cat looking stuck in the tree. Ask children what might happen next. **(Predicting, inferring)**
  - Pause on p5. It looks like Jin is trying to jump up to reach the cat (Slink). Can they tell their talk partner how they might try to rescue the cat? **(Activating prior knowledge)**
  - Ask children to continue reading independently to the end of the story.

After reading

- Return to the text. Use specific praise to comment on individuals who looked carefully at the illustrations to find story clues and to help them tell the story.
- Key skills:
  - Ask children to become detectives. They should look back through the book using their magnifying glass. Ask them to find 5 things that Jin and his family could see on their walk through the park. Challenge the children to 'sound talk'. **(Recall and retrieve, Phase 1: Oral blending and segmenting)**.
  - Ask children why they think the cat (Slink) climbed into the tree. **(Deducing)**
  - Return to p10. Ask children how they think the cat (Slink) is feeling now and why. **(Empathizing)**

Other things to do

- Writing activities
  - Write a list of at least five things Jin and his family could see on his walk through the park. Children could record their list on a digital recording device.
- Speaking, listening and drama
  - Return to p11. Encourage the children to use the small world character puppets and relevant story props to extend the story.
- Cross-curricular links
  - Using PCM 2 ('Make a moving picture'), invite children to make a moving picture of Jin flying. Create new scenes and record them with a simple video camera/tablet. **(Knowledge and Understanding of the World – technology)**

The Lost Cat

Story summary

This is a story about a girl called Pip who helps to find a missing cat (Slink). She does this using her super-strength to lift up a car.

Additional resources: Photocopiable master (PCM) 27: Thought bubble

Phonics and vocabulary checker*

Phonics	
Focus GPCs	a, t, p
Decodable words	tap, pat
Common words	n/a
Common exception/irregular words ('tricky' words)	n/a

Developing vocabulary
Pip, crouching, down, car

The Early Years Foundation Stage Framework**

Early Learning Goals (statutory requirement)		Assessment pointers in this story
ELG 01 Listening and attention	Children give their attention to what others say and respond appropriately, while engaged in another activity.	Check whether children can listen and respond with relevant simple questions when discussing their personal experiences.
ELG 02 Understanding	Children follow instructions involving several ideas or actions.	Check whether children can follow the directions given by peers to locate where the lost cat could be hiding.
ELG 03 Speaking	Children use past, present and future forms accurately when talking about events that have happened or are to happen in the future.	Check children use the correct tenses when extending/creating their own stories.
ELG 09 Reading	Children use phonic knowledge to decode regular words and read them aloud accurately.	Check children use their phonic knowledge as the read the decodable words listed.
	Children demonstrate understanding when talking with others about what they have read.	Check children can talk about how Pip rescued the cat with their talk partners.
ELG 10 Writing	Children use their phonic knowledge to write words in ways which match their spoken sounds.	Check children are using their phonic knowledge to attempt to write simple words on their 'lost' poster.

Oxford Reading Criterion Scale: Assessment Pre-reading Standard

No.	Criteria	Assessment pointers in this story
4	Is beginning to distinguish between sounds in words, particularly initial letter sounds. (READ)	Check the children use their phonic knowledge to read the initial letter sounds in the words: tap, pat.
8	Is beginning to talk about texts, e.g. stating simple likes/ dislikes. (E)	Check children can talk about which parts of the story they liked and disliked.
9	Shows curiosity about content of texts, e.g. may begin to discuss content and answer basic questions about a story (How? Why?). (D)	Check children discuss why they think the cat doesn't want to come out of hiding.
13	Can identify objects that begin with the same sound, e.g. table, tiger, tap. (READ)	Check children can identify objects that start with the sounds: /t/, /p/ and /a/.

*For a full phonic breakdown, see the *Phonic and vocabulary overview* section in this handbook.
**Scottish Curriculum for Excellence/Foundation Phase Framework for Wales/Northern Ireland/Cambridge Primary English and International curricula correlation can be found online at: www.oxfordowl.co.uk

Before reading

- Key skills:
  - Read the title to the children and look at the cover illustration. Involve children in orally blending the word cat. **(Phase 1: Oral blending and segmenting)**
  - Ask children to explain what the word *lost* means. Explain a time when you lost something. Then ask the children if they have ever lost anything. **(Exploring new vocabulary, activating prior knowledge)**
  - Tell children that there are some words in this text. Ask them to flick through the book and point to any words that they see. Explain that the words will help them to read and understand the story. **(Previewing the text)**
- Strategy check:
  - Explain what children should do if they come across a word they don't know how to read. Model using an example from the text.

During reading

- Key skills:
  - Help children decode or understand any difficult words as they are reading independently.
  - Pause on p2. Ask children who they think might be at the door. **(Predicting)**
  - Ask children to describe where the cat is hiding. Encourage the use of positional language.
  - Pause on p6. Ask children why they think the cat doesn't want to come out of hiding. **(Inferring, empathizing)**
  - Praise children in the moment as they recognize the focus GPCs and blend to read the words: *pat, tap.*
  - Pause on p8. It looks like Pip and the cat are both thinking. *I think the cat is thinking…What do you think Pip might be thinking and why?* Use PCM 27 ('Thought bubble') and ask them to share their thoughts verbally. **(Empathizing, inferring)**

After reading

- Return to the text. Check if there were any words that the children found difficult to read and praise effective strategies used by children to read words. Clarify any errors if necessary.
- Key skills:
  - Play *Phoneme detective*: show the children flashcards for the focus GPCs. See if they can locate the phonemes in the words in the text. **(Recall and retrieve)**
  - Ask children to think about where else Slink the cat could have been hiding. Encourage the children to use positional language in their responses. **(Visualizing, making connections with own experiences)**.
  - Ask children to tell their talk partner how Pip rescued the cat. **(Recall and retrieve)**
  - Look back through the book and encourage children to comment on how the lady (Mrs Butterworth's) feelings change as the story progresses. **(Deducing, empathsizing)**

Other things to do

- Writing activities
  - Encourage the children to create their own lost posters for Slink the cat or something that they have lost. Demonstrate segmenting to write the word *lost*.
- Speaking, listening and drama
  - Using PCM 27 ('Thought bubble'), ask children (in pairs) to return to the story and consider what the lady (Mrs Butterworth) and Pip's dad are thinking at the start and the end of the story.
- Cross-curricular links
  - Use small world figures and props associated with the story. Children take it in turns to hide Slink the cat while their friends have to describe where Slink is hiding using positional language. **(Mathematical Development – shape, space and measure)**

Jin's First Day

Story summary

It's Jin's first day at his new school, Hero Academy. The school cat (Slink) takes him on a tour. Jin discovers he's not the only one who has a superpower. He meets Ben and Pip.

Additional resources: Photocopiable master (PCM) 26: Magnifying glass; a memory box containing a photo of the class' first day at school or a note 'think back to your first day at school'; photo of your school building.

Phonics and vocabulary checker*

Phonics	
Focus GPCs	s, a, t, p
Decodable words	tap, pat
Common words	n/a
Common exception/irregular words ('tricky' words)	n/a

Developing vocabulary
Jin, amazed, sight, academy

The Early Years Foundation Stage Framework**

Early Learning Goals (statutory requirement)		Assessment pointers in this story
ELG 01 Listening and attention	Children listen to stories, accurately anticipating key events and respond to what they hear with relevant comments, questions or actions.	Check children can predict what Jin might do on his first day at school.
ELG 02 Understanding	Children answer 'how' and 'why' questions about their experiences and in response to stories or events.	Check children can explain how they were feeling on their first day and why Jin is feeling surprised when he enters Hero Academy (p6).
ELG 03 Speaking	Children develop their own narratives and explanations by connecting ideas or events.	Check children can create their own story based on their first day at school by connecting the ideas and events they remembered.
ELG 09 Reading	Children use phonic knowledge to decode regular words and read them aloud accurately.	Check children use their phonic knowledge as they read the decodable words listed.
	Children demonstrate understanding when talking with others about what they have read.	Check children can discuss the similarities and differences between Hero Academy and their school.
ELG 10 Writing	Children use their phonic knowledge to write words in ways which match their spoken sounds.	Check children are using their phonic (GPC) knowledge to write simple words for their sticky note labels.

Oxford Reading Criterion Scale: Assessment Pre-reading Standard

No.	Criteria	Assessment pointers in this story
7	Can gain simple meaning from texts using illustrations, when not yet able to read the text itself. (D)	Check children understand that this is Jin's first day at a new, special school.
8	Is beginning to talk about texts, e.g. stating simple likes/dislikes. (E)	Check children can talk about which parts of the story they liked and disliked.
13	Can identify objects that begin with the same sound, e.g. table, tiger, tap. (READ)	Check children can identify objects that start with the sounds: /t/, /p/, /s/ and /a/.
18	Is beginning to hear and identify where sounds appear in words. (READ)	Check children can identify the focus GPCs in the story.

*For a full phonic breakdown, see the *Phonic and vocabulary overview* section in this handbook.
**Scottish Curriculum for Excellence/Foundation Phase Framework for Wales/Northern Ireland/Cambridge Primary English and International curricula correlation can be found online at: www.oxfordowl.co.uk

Before reading

- Strategy check:
  - Introduce the children to the memory box (small box/chest) and look at the memory inside. Share either a photo of the children on their first day at school or a note that says 'think back to your first day at school'. Reflect on your own first day at school, sharing details about what you did and how you felt. Invite children to share their own experiences. (Activating prior knowledge)
- Key skills:
  - Look at the cover. Read the title and blurb.
  - Explain to children that we can use our memories to help us predict what Jin might do and understand how he might feel on his first day at school. With their talk partner, ask children to predict two things Jin might do on his first day. (Predicting)
  - Tell children that Jin's school is called Hero Academy. Ask children to explain what *academy* means. Clarify that in this book an *academy* is a special type of school that trains pupils for a particular job. Invite suggestions as to what this might be. (Exploring new vocabulary, activating prior knowledge)
  - Turn to p3. Talk about how Jin is going on a tour of the academy just like they did when they started school. Who is Jin's tour guide? (Previewing text, retrieve)

During reading

- Key skills:
  - Check children remember the strategies they need to use as they are reading the story. Model blending to read unfamiliar words using the word *sat*.
  - Praise children in the moment as they recognize the focus GPCs and blend to read the decodable words listed. Support children who have difficulties decoding words.
  - Pause on p3. Look at the Hero Academy building and a photo of your school building. How is it the same/different to your school? Using PCM 26 (Magnifying glass), challenge the children to be detectives as they read the story to look for clues. (Deducing)
  - Pause on p5. Check children can recognize the keypad lock in the picture. Ask them why they think the building is locked. (Making connections, predicting)
  - Pause on p6. Ask children to explain how Jin is feeling when he enters the building and why. (Empathizing)
  - Ask children to continue reading independently to p11.
  - Pause on p11. Jin has gone into his classroom. Ask children who these people could be. (Inferring)

After reading

- Return to the text. Check that there wasn't anything in the illustrations that puzzled or confused children.
- Key skills:
  - Ask children to describe where Jin visited on his tour of the school in their own words. (Summarizing, recall and retrieve)
  - Ask children to show you which part of the school is their favourite and describe why. (Personal response)
  - Revisit the challenge about how Hero Academy is the same/different to your school. What clues did children find to help you answer this? Share ideas. (Recall and retrieve, inferring)
  - Revisit the idea that Hero Academy is a special type of school that trains children for a particular job. What job might it be? (Deducing)

Other things to do

- Writing activities
  - Tour guide top tips: ask children to think of some tips for showing people round their school. Scribe the children's ideas. Children can add their own drawings/writing where appropriate.
- Speaking, listening and drama
  - *Hot seat* Jin: invite the children to generate and ask questions to find out more about Jin's first day at school.
- Cross-curricular links
  - Can children recall some of the superpowers the other children had in the story? Encourage them to create their own action/movement for each of the superpowers. (Physical Development: moving and handling)

Pip's Prank

Story summary

This is a story about a girl called Pip who uses her super-strength to play a prank on Ben. Pip tricks Ben into thinking a tree has grown at super speed.

Additional resources: Photocopiable master: (PCM) 5: Order the story *Pip's Prank*; image of Pip.

Phonics and vocabulary checker*

Phonics	
Focus GPCs	m, i, d, n
Decodable words	mad, Pip, pit, tips, it, in, is, sit and
Common words	is, it, in, and
Common exception/irregular words ('tricky' words)	n/a

Developing vocabulary
prank, Ben, Slink

The Early Years Foundation Stage Framework**

Early Learning Goals (statutory requirement)		Assessment pointers in this story
ELG 01 Listening and attention	Children listen to stories, accurately anticipating key events and respond to what they hear with relevant comments, questions or actions.	Check children can locate where in the text it explains how Ben is feeling. (text and image clues)
ELG 02 Understanding	Children answer 'how' and 'why' questions about their experiences and in response to stories or events.	Check children understand how Pip tricked Ben and why he was mad.
ELG 03 Speaking	Children develop their own narratives and explanations by connecting ideas or events.	Check children can use the story map on p12 to retell the story in their own words.
ELG 09 Reading	Children use phonic knowledge to decode regular words and read them aloud accurately.	Check children can recall the focus GPCs as they read decodable words listed.
	Children read and understand simple sentences.	Check children can blend unfamiliar words in order to read simple sentences.
ELG 10 Writing	Children write simple sentences which can be read by themselves and others. Some words are spelt correctly and others are phonetically plausible.	Check children have written at least one simple sentence for their story map making phonetically plausible attempts at some words and spelling some correctly.

Oxford Reading Criterion Scale: Assessment Standard 1

No.	Criteria	Assessment pointers in this story
1	Can distinguish between a word, a letter and a space. (READ)	Check children can read simple sentences.
2	Can understand the terms: book, cover, beginning, middle, end, page, word, letter, line. (READ)	Check children can locate the title of the book on the cover and can understand some book terminology.
6	Is able to read some words from the YR high-frequency word list. (READ)	Check children can read the common words listed.
7	Can state simple likes/dislikes about familiar texts. (E)	Check children can say which part of the story they liked/disliked and why.

*For a full phonic breakdown, see the *Phonic and vocabulary overview* section in this handbook.
**Scottish Curriculum for Excellence/Foundation Phase Framework for Wales/Northern Ireland/Cambridge Primary English and International curricula correlation can be found online at: www.oxfordowl.co.uk

Before reading

- Key skills:
  - Share an image of Pip. Have children met this character before? Write Pip's name with a phoneme/sound button under each letter. Count the phonemes. Remind children how to say each phoneme as they press the button and blend to read the word. **(Recall, making connections, word reading)**
  - Look at the front cover and read the title/blurb. Discuss the word *prank*. Explain the word and provide an example within a sentence. **(Exploring new vocabulary)**
  - Turn to p2 and read 'In this story'. Ask children who Pip might play a prank on and how she might use her super strength. **(Predicting, previewing the text)**
  - Turn to p3 and read *pit* together. Check that they understand that a pit is another word for a hole. **(Exploring new vocabulary)**
- Strategy check:
  - Show the children the sentence *Pip taps it* written on a whiteboard. Explain that this book includes some words grouped into short sentences with finger spaces used to separate the words. Model blending to read each word in turn. Return to the beginning to reread the sentence for sense. **(Word reading, fluency)**

During reading

- Key skills:
  - Check children remember the strategies they need to use as they are reading the story. **(Word reading).**
  - Pause on p5. It looks like Pip is hiding from Ben. Ask children what Ben has been doing so far. **(Recall and retrieve, summarizing)**
  - Praise children in the moment as they recognize the focus GPCs and blend them to read each word in order to read simple sentences. Support and note children who have difficulties decoding words in isolation or to read simple sentences.
  - Pause on p10. Ask children why Ben sprays Pip with the hose. **(Inferring)**
  - Ask children to continue reading independently to the end of the story.

After reading

- Return to the text. Check if there were any words that the children found difficult to read and praise effective strategies used by children to read words. Clarify any errors if necessary.
- Key skills:
  - Give each child a copy of the six story pictures from PCM 5 ('Order the story: *Pip's Prank*'). Can they order the story in the correct sequence to make their own story map? Ask individuals to tell you what happened in specific parts of the story in their own words. **(Summarizing)**
  - Return to p8–9. Ask children how they know how Ben is feeling? Can they show you in the story? **(Recall and retrieve)**
  - Think back to the predictions children made about who Pip was going to play a prank on. Were they correct? Can they tell a talk partner about the prank Pip played on Ben? Can they talk about a prank they have played on someone? **(Summarizing, activating prior knowledge, making connections)**

Other things to do

- Writing activities
  - Ask children to help Ben to write some instructions for planting seeds. Acting as scribe, help the children to plan the instructions looking back at what Ben did in the story and making connections with their own experiences.
- Speaking, listening and drama
  - Role play garden centre or shop: encourage the children to adopt appropriate roles and connect ideas as they play using what they know and understand in their play.
- Cross-curricular links
  - Read the instructions on a seed packet and help the children to plant seeds in the outdoor area or in a seed tray. Can they follow a set of simple instructions? **(Understanding the World – the world)**

It is a Tip

Story summary

In this story, the heroes create a mess in the science room (lab). Mrs Molten is cross and her superpower causes her to overheat. Magnus and Ben come to the rescue.

Additional resources: Photocopiable master (PCM) 6: Complete the sentence; PCM 28: Feelings fan; sticky notes and pencils.

Phonics and vocabulary checker*

Phonics	
Focus GPCs	m, i, d, n
Decodable words	mad, mat, it, is, tip, Pip, tin, sit, sip, and, sad, pan
Common words	is, it, a, and
Common exception/irregular words ('tricky' words)	n/a

Developing vocabulary
tip (mess), tip (move/direction), pan, Ben, Mrs Molten, Magnus, Slink

The Early Years Foundation Stage Framework**

Early Learning Goals (statutory requirement)		Assessment pointers in this story
ELG 01 Listening and attention	Children give their attention to what others say and respond appropriately, while engaged in another activity.	Check children listen and respond to each other, giving eye contact when they are discussing their favourite part of the story.
ELG 02 Understanding	Children answer 'how' and 'why' questions about their experiences and in response to stories or events.	Check children can recall how the class help to tidy up the science lab and understand why Mrs Molten was cross.
ELG 03 Speaking	Children express themselves effectively, showing awareness of listeners' needs.	Check children can express their ideas about how Mrs Molten's feelings changed through the story.
ELG 09 Reading	Children use phonic knowledge to decode regular words and read them aloud accurately.	Check children can recognize the focus GPCs as they recall the decodable words listed.
	Children demonstrate understanding when talking with others about what they have read.	Check children can explain how Ben and Magnus help Mrs Molten.
ELG 10 Writing	Children write simple sentences which can be read by themselves and others. Some words are spelt correctly and others are phonetically plausible.	Check children can use their phonic knowledge to make signs for Mrs Molten's science lab making phonetically plausible attempts at longer words or words.

Oxford Reading Criterion Scale: Assessment Standard 1

No.	Criteria	Assessment pointers in this story
3	When prompted, can use illustrations to support talk about what is happening in a text and to predict what might happen next. (D)	Check children can predict what might happen when Magnus tells Ben to get the pan (p8).
5	Can use developing GPC knowledge to sound and blend simple VC and CVC words. (READ)	Check children can recognize the focus GPCs and read the decodable and common words in the story.
11	Can point to a full stop in text. (READ)	Check children can point to the full stops on p4, p6, p10 and p11.
12	Can retell familiar stories with growing confidence. (R)	Check children can retell the story using the story map on p12.

*For a full phonic breakdown, see the *Phonic and vocabulary overview* section in this handbook.
**Scottish Curriculum for Excellence/Foundation Phase Framework for Wales/Northern Ireland/Cambridge Primary English and International curricula correlation can be found online at: www.oxfordowl.co.uk

Before reading

- Key skills:
  - Use flashcards to run through the focus GPCs. Tell children that they will spot the GPCs in some of the words they will read in the story. Give each child a focus phoneme and explain that they have one minute against the timer to look through the book to spot their target GPC in words.
  - Look at the illustration on the front cover and invite the children to read the title. Draw their attention to the exclamation mark, which tells us that the author would like us to read the sentence to show emotion (surprise or shock in this example). Model this for the children. **(Word reading, fluency)**
  - Discuss and clarify the meaning of the word *tip*. **(Exploring new vocabulary)**
  - Talk about a day when the school was a tip, e.g. *I remember when the playground was a tip. The wind had blown the bin …* Ask children to tell you about a time when their bedroom/house was a tip. **(Activating prior knowledge, making connections)**
  - Look at p3. Where is this story set? Check children have the vocabulary to talk about the science classroom/laboratory. **(Previewing the text)**

During reading

- Key skills:
  - Challenge children to jot down on a sticky note any words that they find that include the target GPC you give each of them. Model this if necessary.
  - Pause on p2. Talk about the characters in the story. Introduce any new characters (orally segment *Molten* and *Magnus*. **(Activating prior knowledge, recall and retrieve)**
  - Pause after reading p4 and p5. Ask children to describe how Mrs Molten is feeling. How can they tell from the text? **(Empathizing, locating information)**
  - Praise children 'in the moment' as they recognize the focus GPCs and blend to read each word, in the simple sentences. Support and note children who have difficulties.
  - Look at p7. Discuss what Ben might be saying to Magnus. **(Inferring)**
  - Ask children to explain in their own words how Magnus and Ben help Mrs Molten. **(Summarizing)**
  - Ask children to continue reading independently to the end of the story.

After reading

- Return to the text. Check if there were any words that the children found difficult to read and praise effective strategies used by individuals to read words.
- Key skills:
  - Return to p11. Ask children if Mrs Molten was still mad/cross at the end of the story. Introduce the children to PCM 28 ('Feelings fan'). Explain that this will help them to think about a range of feelings not just being happy or sad. **(Deducing, empathizing)**
  - Talk about/make a list of the jobs that the characters are doing when tidying up. **(Recall and retrieve)**
  - Ask children to share their favourite part of the story with a talk partner. Model if necessary. **(Personal response)**

Other things to do

- Writing activities
  - Using PCM 6 ('Complete the sentence'), invite the children to recall each event from the story. Encourage them to reread each sentence to check that it makes sense and connects with the event in the picture.
- Speaking, listening and drama
  - Return to p6. Look at the text in the speech bubble. Remind the children that Mrs Molten is feeling cross. How do they think Mrs Molten would say: 'It is a tip!'? Explain that when they speak they should change their voice and pretend to be cross like Mrs Molten. **(Fluency)**
- Cross-curricular links
  - Ask children to think about the rules you have about keeping your classroom tidy. **(Personal, Social and Emotional – managing feelings and behaviour)**

Cat in a Cap

Story summary

In this story, Pip gets a sewing kit and makes a spotty outfit for Slink the cat. Slink isn't keen and tries to hide. Pip uses her super-strength to reach Slink.

Additional resources: Photocopiable master (PCM) 7: Slink's outfit; PCM 28: Feelings fan; craft/sewing kit equipment.

Phonics and vocabulary checker*

Phonics	
Focus GPCs	g, o, c, k
Decodable words	got, gap, pom-poms, spots, not, on, cod, can, cat, cap, cod, kit, skids
Common words	on, can, got, not
Common exception/irregular words ('tricky' words)	n/a

Developing vocabulary
pom-poms, gap, skids, Slink

The Early Years Foundation Stage Framework**

Early Learning Goals (statutory requirement)		Assessment pointers in this story
ELG 01 Listening and attention	Children listen to stories, accurately anticipating key events and respond to what they hear with relevant comments, questions or actions.	Check children can recall and describe the outfit Pip is going to make for Slink.
ELG 02 Understanding	Children answer 'how' and 'why' questions about their experiences and in response to stories or events.	Check children understand why Slink's mood has changed at the end of the story and if they inferred how Pip would use her superpower (p7).
ELG 03 Speaking	Children use past, present and future forms accurately when talking about events that have happened or are to happen in the future.	Check children use the correct tense as they retell the story in their own words.
ELG 09 Reading	Children read and understand simple sentences.	Check children can read simple sentences: *Pip got a kit*; *Pip can tip it*.
	Children demonstrate understanding when talking with others about what they have read.	Check children can predict how Pip will use her superpower to retrieve Slink.
ELG 10 Writing	Children write simple sentences which can be read by themselves and others. Some words are spelt correctly and others are phonetically plausible.	Check children can use their own writing/drawings to record something they made using a craft kit.

Oxford Reading Criterion Scale: Assessment Standard 1

No.	Criteria	Assessment pointers in this story
4	Can sequence the important parts of a story that is known to the reader in order. (R)	Check children can retell key events from the story in order.
6	Is able to read some words from the YR high-frequency word list. (READ)	Check children can read the common words listed.
7	Can state simple likes/dislikes about familiar texts. (E)	Check children can talk about which parts of the story they liked and disliked.
11	Can point to a full stop in text. (READ)	Check children can point to the full stops on p3, p7, p8, p9, and p11.

*For a full phonic breakdown, see the *Phonic and vocabulary overview* section in this handbook.
**Scottish Curriculum for Excellence/Foundation Phase Framework for Wales/Northern Ireland/Cambridge Primary English and International curricula correlation can be found online at: www.oxfordowl.co.uk

Before reading

- Strategy check:
  - Practise recalling the focus GPCs. Write a sentence from the text on the whiteboard. Ask children how many words there are. How do we know where each word starts/ends? Model blending to read each word in turn. Can they spot the focus GPCs in the words?
- Key skills:
  - Look at the front and back cover. Read the title/blurb and look at the illustrations. Ask children who they think this story is about. How can we check this? (Page 2 tells us which characters are in this story). **(Predicting)**
  - The blurb says 'Pip gets a kit'. Talk about what the word 'kit' means. Discuss what type of kit it might be and what she might do with it. **(Previewing the text)**
  - Turn to p3. The author has added a label to give us more information. Can children name the tools and equipment that are in Pip's kit? (Wool/scissors/needle/thread/fabric). **(Exploring new vocabulary)**
  - Talk about how you once got a craft kit to make a ... Ask children *if they have ever had a craft kit like Pip's and if so can they tell you what they made with it?* **(Activating prior knowledge, making connections)**

During reading

- Key skills:
  - Help children to decode or understand difficult words as they are reading independently.
  - Give specific 'in the moment' praise as individuals say the phonemes that they see and then blend them together to hear an unfamiliar word. **(Word reading)**
  - Ask if anyone can recall what Pip's superpower is from a previous story, e.g. *The Lost Cat.* **(Activating prior knowledge)**
  - Pause on p4. Ask children to describe the outfit Pip is planning to make for Slink. (Note which children refer to the labels and illustration to help them). How many pom-poms are on the cap? **(Recall and retrieve)**
  - Pause on p7. Ask children how Pip might use her superpower to find Slink. **(Predicting, inferring)**

After reading

- Return to the text. Were there any words that they couldn't read or didn't understand? It might be appropriate to discuss reading words with adjacent consonants: skids/Slink. **(Word reading)**
- Key skills:
  - Return to p5. Remind the children that the words in a thought bubble tell us what a character is thinking. Ask children if they think that Slink is excited about Pip's plan for his new outfit. **(Empathizing)**
  - Ask children if they can think of anywhere else in the classroom that Sink could hide. **(Inferring)**
  - Talk about why Slink's mood has changed at the end of the story. **(Deducing)**
  - Ask the children to use the story map on p12 to retell the story in their own words. **(Summarizing)**

Other things to do

- Writing activities
  - Using PCM 7 ('Slink's outfit'), blend to read each label. Add the labels to Slink's new superhero outfit.
- Speaking, listening and drama
  - Using PCM 28 ('Feelings fan') ask children to reread the story with a friend. Get them to stop and show how Slink's feelings change, saying why.
- Cross-curricular links
  - Design your own outfit for Slink and write labels like the design on p4 of the story. **(Expressive Arts and Design)**

Stop, Cat!

Story summary

There's a surprise birthday party for Slink the cat. Disaster strikes when Slink is lifted into the air by a balloon. Jin comes to his rescue.

Additional resources: Photocopiable master (PCM) 25: Speech bubble; PCM 27: Thought bubble; a memory box – a photo of a birthday party, birthday card/badge.

Phonics and vocabulary checker*

Phonics	
Focus GPCs	g o, c, k
Decodable words	gas, gasp, got, cod, top, stop, got, pop, can, cat, cod, kit
Common words	on, can, got, not
Common exception/irregular words ('tricky' words)	n/a

Developing vocabulary
nap, gasp, kit, Jin, Slink,

The Early Years Foundation Stage Framework**

Early Learning Goals (statutory requirement)		Assessment pointers in this story
ELG 01 Listening and attention	Children give their attention to what others say and respond appropriately, while engaged in another activity.	Check children can listen to each other's ideas as they infer what Slink was thinking (p8).
ELG 02 Understanding	Children answer 'how' and 'why' questions about their experiences and in response to stories or events.	Check children can predict how Jin might rescue Slink and deduce why Pip popped the balloon.
ELG 03 Speaking	Children express themselves effectively, showing awareness of listeners' needs.	Check children can use expression as they infer what Slink is thinking (p8).
ELG 09 Reading	Children use phonic knowledge to decode regular words and read them aloud accurately.	Check children can blend to read words containing the focus GPCs.
	Children demonstrate understanding when talking with others about what they have read.	Check children can make connections between their own experiences (birthday parties) and Slink's party.
ELG 10 Writing	Children use their phonic knowledge to write words in ways which match their spoken sounds.	Check children use their phonic knowledge to make birthday cards/pictures for Slink segmenting and writing taught GPCs.

Oxford Reading Criterion Scale: Assessment Standard 1

No.	Criteria	Assessment pointers in this story
2	Can understand the terms: book, cover, beginning, middle, end, page, word, letter, line. (READ)	Children understand and can talk about the different parts of the story.
5	Can use developing GPC knowledge to sound and blend simple VC and CVC words. (READ)	Check children can blend to read the decodable words listed that contain the focus GPCs.
18	With support, can find information to help answer simple, literal questions. (R)	Check children can answer questions about Slink, e.g. What was Slink doing at the start of the story?
20	Can talk about main points or key events in a simple text. (R)	Ask children to retell the story using the story map on p12.

*For a full phonic breakdown, see the *Phonic and vocabulary overview* section in this handbook.
**Scottish Curriculum for Excellence/Foundation Phase Framework for Wales/Northern Ireland/Cambridge Primary English and International curricula correlation can be found online at: www.oxfordowl.co.uk

Before reading

- Key skills:
  - Look at the cover and ask children to read the title. Ask children why the heroes might want to stop the cat. Ask them to recall any other stories they've read where Slink is featured. **(Predicting, activating prior knowledge)**
  - Turn to p2. Discuss who the main characters in the story are. **(Recall and retrieve)**
  - Clarify the meaning of the context vocabulary listed in the *Developing vocabulary* box opposite. **(Exploring new vocabulary)**
- Strategy check:
  - Ask children to locate any labels, though bubbles or speech bubbles in the story. Briefly recap on the purpose of each. **(Previewing the text, fluency)**
  - Remind the children that good readers make connections between their personal experiences. Reveal the memory box. Talk about a birthday party you remember (what you did, your favourite present, how you felt). Invite the children to join in with their own experiences. **(Activating prior knowledge)**
  - Practise recall of the focus GPCs and blend to read the decodable words listed.

During reading

- Key skills:
  - Check children remember the strategies they need to use as they are reading the story. **(Word reading)**.
  - Pause on p2. Do children think Slink is feeling happy that Jin has woken him up? **(Empathizing)**
  - Pause on p4. Look at the banner. Get children to think about what it might say. **(Predicting, word reading: environmental print)**
  - Praise children 'in the moment' as they recognize the focus GPCs and blend to read each word in the simple sentences. Support and note children who have difficulties.
  - Pause on p6. Pip and Jin give Slink presents. Ask children how the characters feel about Slink. **(Inferring)**
  - Pause on p8. Ask children to explain to their talk partner what has happened to Slink. Do they have any ideas about how to rescue Slink?
  - Pause on p11. Ask children why they think Pip decided to pop Slink's birthday balloon. **(Deducing)**

After reading

- Return to the text. Check if there were any words that the children found difficult to read and praise effective strategies used to read new words. Clarify any errors if necessary.
- Key skills:
  - Return to p7. Look carefully at the illustration. Ask children if there are any clues to suggest that Slink's birthday party was a surprise. (Slink has a shocked/ surprised expression). **(Inferring, deducing)**
  - Return to p7 and p8. Talk about the different party food. Which do children think is Slink's favourite? (cod). Discuss their favourite party foods. Scribe a list of the group's favourites. **(Recall and retrieve, making connections)**
  - Ask children to create a picture in their heads of a birthday party they remember. Is Slink's birthday party like the one they remember? Discuss similarities/differences. **(Visualizing in order to respond)**
  - Return to p8. Use PCM 25 ('Speech bubbles') or PCM 27 ('Thought bubble') to suggest what Slink might be saying or thinking as the balloon is lifting higher into the sky. **(Inferring)**

Other things to do

- Writing activities
  - Invite the children to make birthday cards/pictures for Slink.
- Speaking, listening and drama
  - Create a birthday party role play corner. Invite the children to set the home corner for a birthday party and create their own birthday party stories as they play.
- Cross-curricular links
  - Slink was lifted into the air by the balloon because he was so light. Investigate which objects are heavier/lighter than Slink (using a cuddly toy cat). **(Mathematics – shape, space and measure)**

Tuck In

Story summary

Magnus gives Slink his favourite food for lunch but a rat decides to run off with it. Disaster strikes when Slink skids into a lunch table as he tries to retrieve it.

Additional resources: Photocopiable master (PCM) 9: Action words; PCM 26: Magnifying glass; PCM 27: Thought bubble.

Phonics and vocabulary checker*

Phonics	
Focus GPCs	ck, e, u, r
Decodable words	kick, tuck, picks, gets, get, pet, Magnus, runs, up, rat
Common words	get, up
Common exception/irregular words ('tricky' words)	to, the

Developing vocabulary
Magnus, Slink, tuck in, skids

The Early Years Foundation Stage Framework**

Early Learning Goals (statutory requirement)		Assessment pointers in this story
ELG 01 Listening and attention	Children give their attention to what others say and respond appropriately, while engaged in another activity.	Check children are listening carefully to what others say as they discuss Magnus' thoughts.
ELG 02 Understanding	Children answer 'how' and 'why' questions about their experiences and in response to stories or events.	Check children are able to explain how Magnus solves the problem at the end of the story and why Slink tries to use his superpower.
ELG 03 Speaking	Children develop their own narratives and explanations by connecting ideas or events.	Check children are able to explain how Slink's feelings change by connecting events through the story.
ELG 09 Reading	Children read and understand simple sentences.	Check children recognize the focus GPCs and blend them to read the decodable words in the story.
	Children use phonic knowledge to decode regular words and read them aloud accurately.	Check children can blend unfamiliar words in order to read simple sentences.
ELG 10 Writing	Children write simple sentences which can be read by themselves and others. Some words are spelt correctly and others are phonetically plausible.	Check children understand how to construct a simple sentence to label their pet drawing.

Oxford Reading Criterion Scale: Assessment Standard 1

No.	Criteria	Assessment pointers in this story
4	Can sequence the important parts of a story that is known to the reader in order. (R)	Check children can talk about what happened first, next etc.
5	Can use developing GPC knowledge to sound and blend simple VC and CVC words. (READ)	Check children recognize the focus GPCs and blend to read the decodable words listed.
6	Is able to read some words from the YR high-frequency word list. (READ)	Check children can read the common/common exception words listed.
7	Can state simple likes/dislikes about familiar texts. (E)	Check children can talk about which bits of the story they liked and disliked.

*For a full phonic breakdown, see the *Phonic and vocabulary overview* section in this handbook.
**Scottish Curriculum for Excellence/Foundation Phase Framework for Wales/Northern Ireland/Cambridge Primary English and International curricula correlation can be found online at: www.oxfordowl.co.uk

Before reading

- Key skills:
  - Look at the cover illustrations and read the title. Clarify what the phrase 'tuck in' might mean in this book.
  - Look at p2. Talk about the main characters in the book. Encourage children to read the caption 'Slink can kick'. **(Previewing the text)**
  - Read the blurb. Check children understand the word *cod*. Talk about why Slink might need to get his cod back.
  - Remind children that good readers make connections with what they already know to help them understand what they are reading. Ask them what they already know about Slink. What might his favourite food be. **(Activating prior knowledge, predicting)**
- Strategy check:
  - Look at the focus GPCs. Remind the children that 'ck' is a digraph where two letters are used to represent one phoneme /ck/ as in duck. The phoneme (sound) will be familiar to them; it is the grapheme (way it is written) that looks different. Show them the word '*tuck*' using phoneme buttons. Count the phonemes. This will help us to remember that we say /ck/ not /c/ /k/ when. **(Word reading)**
  - Turn to p5. There are two sentences on this page. Ask children to show you with their fingers the order they will read them in. Clarify any misconceptions relating to direction. **(Fluency)**

During reading

- Key skills:
  - Ask children to be phoneme detectives: can they use their magnifying glass (PCM 26) to look for words that contain the digraph 'ck' and note them on their whiteboards? **(Word reading)**
  - Pause on p4. Help the children to read the tricky word *the*. Explain that we say it is tricky because we don't know how to say the GPCs yet to blend it so we will try to learn to recognize this word when we see it.
  - Pause before reading p4. Ask children what is happening in the illustration. Note both the drink spillage and the rat stealing the cod.
  - Pause on p5. What new information does the text tell us? **(Recall and retrieve)**
  - Pause before reading p7. Help the children to read the tricky word '*to*'. Explain that we say it is tricky because in this word the 'o' represents a different phoneme.
  - Pause after reading p7. Look at Magnus' facial expression. Ask children why he looks this way. What is he thinking. **(Predicting, inferring, empathizing)**
  - Pause on p11. Mention that this page looks familiar. Have we seen it before? **(Recall and retrieve)**

After reading

- Return to the text. Check if there were any words that the children found difficult to read and praise effective strategies used. Clarify any errors if necessary.
- Key skills:
  - Return to p10. Ask children what Slink is thinking when Magnus explains that the rat is a pet. Encourage the group to use their thought bubbles (PCM 27) to share Slink's thoughts. **(Inferring)**
  - Ask children to discuss with their talk partners how Magnus solves the problem at the end of the story. **(Summarizing)**
  - Talk about Slink's feelings and how they changed. Do children feel sorry for Slink in this story? **(Personal response)**

Other things to do

- Writing activities
  - Using PCM 9 (Action words), ask children to choose the correct action word to complete each sentence. Cut up sentences and reread them. Locate the illustration in the book that they match to.
- Speaking, listening and drama
  - Hero Academy role play: children take on the roles of their favourite characters as they re-enact the story.
- Cross-curricular links
  - Use non-fiction books or online video clips to learn more about pet rats. Ask children to write some instructions about caring for them. Adult to scribe. **(Understanding of the World – the world)**

Magnus is Stuck

Story summary

It is a windy day. A gust of wind lifts Magnus into the air and he becomes stuck in a tree. Pip uses her super-strength to rescue Magnus.

Additional resources: Photocopiable master (PCM) 28: Feelings fan; sticky notes or Hero Academy bookmarks (p17 of this handbook).

Phonics and vocabulary checker*

Phonics	
Focus GPCs	ck, e, u, r
Decodable words	pick, picks, rock, rocks, sack, stuck, get, gets, Magnus, gust, stuck, runs
Common words	get, up
Common exception/irregular words ('tricky' words)	to, the

Developing vocabulary
Magnus, sack, gust

The Early Years Foundation Stage Framework**

Early Learning Goals (statutory requirement)		Assessment pointers in this story
ELG 01 Listening and attention	Children listen to stories, accurately anticipating key events and respond to what they hear with relevant comments, questions or actions.	Check children can predict what might happen to Magnus and whether they can suggest how Magnus might feel.
ELG 02 Understanding	Children follow instructions involving several ideas or actions.	Check children can follow instructions as they read on their own locating common exception words listed.
ELG 03 Speaking	Children use past, present and future forms accurately when talking about events that have happened or are to happen in the future.	Check children are able to use the past tense when they recall what happened to Magnus.
ELG 09 Reading	Children use phonic knowledge to decode regular words and read them aloud accurately.	Check the children recognize the focus GPCs and blend to read the decodable words listed.
	They also read some common irregular words.	Check children are able to read by sight the common exception words listed.
ELG 10 Writing	They also write some irregular common words.	Check children write the common exception word *the* in their windy day weather pictures.

Oxford Reading Criterion Scale: Assessment Standard 1

No.	Criteria	Assessment pointers in this story
3	When prompted, can use illustrations to support talk about what is happening in a text and to predict what might happen next. (D)	Check children talk about the weather in the story and what time of year it might be.
5	Can use developing GPC knowledge to sound and blend simple VC and CVC words. (READ)	Check children recognize the focus GPCs and blend them to read the decodable words in the story.
8	Can talk about the main points/key events in a text, e.g. main story setting, events, principle character. (R)	Check children can retell the story using the story map on p12.
11	Can point to a full stop in text. (READ)	Check children can point to the full stops on p2, p4, p7, p8, p9, p10, and p11.

*For a full phonic breakdown, see the *Phonic and vocabulary overview* section in this handbook.
**Scottish Curriculum for Excellence/Foundation Phase Framework for Wales/Northern Ireland/Cambridge Primary English and International curricula correlation can be found online at: www.oxfordowl.co.uk

Before reading

- Key skills:
  - Look at the front and back cover. Read the title and blurb. Check children understand what is meant by the word '*stuck*' in this context. Discuss their own experiences of being stuck.
  - Talk about your memories of a windy day, e.g. *I remember a really windy day when my washing blew off the line*. Ask them to tell you about a time when it was windy. What was it like? **(Activating prior knowledge)**
  - Turn to p4. Check children know what Magnus is holding and locate the word '*sack*' in the written text. Clarify its purpose and what Magnus is using it for. **(Exploring new vocabulary, predicting, activating prior knowledge)**
- Strategy check:
  - Practise reading the common exception words listed written on a mini-whiteboard. Remind children that these are words that we can't yet segment so we are trying to recognize these when we see them. Challenge them to look out for these words as they read and use sticky notes or their bookmarks to mark where they locate them. **(Word reading)**

During reading

- Key skills:
  - Pause on p3. What can children tell you about the weather in this picture? What clues are there? **(Making connections, inferring)**
  - Pause on p4. Discuss what might happen next. **(Predicting)**
  - Praise children 'in the moment' as they recognize the focus GPCs, blend to read each word in the simple sentences. Support and note children who have difficulties.
  - Pause on p5. Check children understand what a *gust* is. *A sudden strong rush of wind*.
  - Pause on p6. Look at Pip's facial expression. Can they use the feelings fan (PCM 28) to suggest how Pip is feeling? **(Empathizing, predicting)**
  - Pause on p7. In one minute, can they tell their talk partner what has happened in the story so far. Note whether children are recalling details or returning to the text to retrieve information. **(Summarizing, recall and retrieve)**
  - Pause on p11. Ask children how Pip used her scarf to release Magnus from the tree. Introduce the children to the term *lasso* to help them understand what Pip did. **(Recall and retrieve, summarizing)**

After reading

- Return to the text. Invite children to show examples of the common exception words that they located during reading. Clarify any errors if necessary. **(Word reading)**
- Key skills:
  - Return to p7. Encourage children to use the feelings fan (PCM 28) to show how Magnus is feeling and then consider how they would feel if they were stuck in a tree. Help them by scribing their feelings. **(Empathizing, inferring)**
  - Ask children if they were surprised by how Pip rescued Magnus. If they were Pip, what would they have done? **(Recall and retrieve, personal response)**

Other things to do

- Writing activities
  - Ask children to draw a windy day picture, labelling some of the things that they might spot blowing in the wind.
- Speaking, listening and drama
  - Go on a 'windy day walk'. Recall the clues we noticed in the story that told us it was a windy day. Talk about how it feels to be out on a windy day. What do they notice?
- Cross-curricular links
  - Provide a 'windy day resource box' in the outdoor area for children to explore including kites, ribbons, streamers, bubble machine, balloons, flags, wind mills and wind chimes. Encourage the children to investigate which way the wind is blowing, how strong the wind is and explore the sounds made by the wind chimes. **(Understanding the World – the world)**

Jin is Ill

Story summary

Jin is feeling unwell and Mrs Butterworth sends him to bed to rest with a mug of hot lemon. The next day Jin is feeling better but Ben is not well!

Additional resources: Photocopiable master (PCM) 25: Speech bubble.

Phonics and vocabulary checker*

Phonics	
Focus GPCs	h, b, f, l, ff, ll, ss
Decodable words	hot, hop, Ben, bad, bug, back, bed, fan, fun, fuss, luck, lemon, off, ill
Common words	of, off, back, big
Common exception/irregular words ('tricky' words)	no, go, I

Developing vocabulary
Jin, Mrs Butterworth, bug (illness), lemon

The Early Years Foundation Stage Framework**

Early Learning Goals (statutory requirement)		Assessment pointers in this story
ELG 01 Listening and attention	Children listen to stories, accurately anticipating key events and respond to what they hear with relevant comments, questions or actions.	Check children are able to comment upon their own experiences of feeling ill and link this to how Jin is feeling in the story.
ELG 02 Understanding	Children answer 'how' and 'why' questions about their experiences and in response to stories or events.	Check children can explain how Mrs Butterworth helped Jin and why she made him go to bed.
ELG 03 Speaking	Children develop their own narratives and explanations by connecting ideas or events.	Check children can create their own role play story about being ill by connecting events.
ELG 09 Reading	Children read and understand simple sentences.	Check children understand what is wrong with Jin after reading the text on p3.
	Children use phonic knowledge to decode regular words and read them aloud accurately.	Check children recognize the focus GPCs and blend them to read the decodable words in the story.
ELG 10 Writing	Children write simple sentences which can be read by themselves and others. Some words are spelt correctly and others are phonetically plausible.	Check children use their phonic knowledge to write a message inside Ben's get well soon card.

Oxford Reading Criterion Scale: Assessment Standard 1

No.	Criteria	Assessment pointers in this story
6	Is able to read some words from the YR high-frequency word list. (READ)	Check children can read the common words in the story.
7	Can state simple likes/dislikes about familiar texts. (E)	Check children can talk about which parts of the story they liked and disliked.
10	Knows a wider range of GPCs and can sound and blend to read most CVC words (including words with double letters, e.g. bell, hiss). (READ)	Check children recognize the focus GPCs and blend them to read the decodable words in the story.
12	Can retell familiar stories with growing confidence. (R)	Check children can retell the story using the story map on p12.

*For a full phonic breakdown, see the *Phonic and vocabulary overview* section in this handbook.
**Scottish Curriculum for Excellence/Foundation Phase Framework for Wales/Northern Ireland/Cambridge Primary English and International curricula correlation can be found online at: www.oxfordowl.co.uk

Before reading

Practise reading the common exception words listed.

* Key skills:
  * Look at the front and back cover. Read the title and blurb together. Notice the focus phoneme /ll/ in the word *ill*. Check the children understand the meaning of the word *ill*. **(Exploring new vocabulary)**
  * Turn to p3. Draw the children's attention to the thermometer and discuss how it is used when someone is ill. Encourage the children to draw upon their own experiences. **(Activating prior knowledge, making connections)**
  * Ask children what they think might make Jin feel better. How will Mrs Butterworth help Jin? **(Predicting)**
* Strategy check:
  * Draw children's attention to the speech bubbles used in the story (hold up PCM 25: 'Speech bubble'), and remind them that when they are reading the text in a speech bubble they should try to change their voice and add expression so that they sound like the character would. Model reading Jin on p3. Explain that you will be listening to see who is doing this as they read on their own. **(Fluency)**

During reading

* Key skills:
  * Pause on p4. Ask children why Mrs Butterworth has switched the fan on. **(Inferring)**
  * Praise the children 'in the moment' as they blend to read words containing the focus digraphs ll, ff, and ss. Support children who don't recognize that the two letters in these words are making one phoneme (sound) not two. **(Word reading)**
  * Pause on p5. Praise children who use a cross voice to read 'Get off!'. Ask children why Mrs Butterworth has shooed Slink off the bed. **(Activating prior knowledge, making connections)**
  * Pause on p7. Ask children why Jin looks fed up. How would they feel if they had to stay in bed? **(Empathizing)**
  * Ask children to continue reading independently to the end of the story on p11.

After reading

* Return to the text. Check if there were any words that the children found difficult to read. Invite a child or demonstrate yourself how to chop the word up into syllables *lem/on* and blend them before putting them back together. **(Word reading)**
* Key skills:
  * Ben goes to visit Jin. Ask children what he takes with him. If they were feeling ill what might make them feel better? **(Recall and retrieve, making connections)**
  * Mrs Butterworth looked after both Jin and Ben when they were feeling poorly. Ask children what she did to help them in the story. **(Deducing, personal response)**
  * Return to p11. Encourage the children to think about what might happen next. **(Predicting)**

Other things to do

* Writing activities
  * Invite children to make 'get well soon' cards or pictures for Ben in the story. Ask them to think about what picture might make Ben feel better.
* Speaking, listening and drama
  * Encourage children to do a Hero Academy role play with doctor's kit props. Ask children to imagine that all the pupils at Hero Academy catch Jin's bug. Who might be ill? What is wrong with them? How will Mrs Butterworth help them?
* Cross-curricular links
  * Discuss ways of keeping healthy that would help them to stay well. Children could also make posters, e.g. to remind their friends to wash their hands and cover their mouths when they are sneezing. **(Physical Development – health and self-care)**

Ben Helps

Story summary

Ben wants to help Miss Baker in the kitchen with her jobs but things start to go wrong when he tries to rush! He learns that his superpower isn't always helpful.

Additional resources: Photocopiable master (PCM) 28: Feelings fan; PCM 30: Splat mat.

Phonics and vocabulary checker*

Phonics	
Focus GPCs	h, b, f, l, ff, ll, ss
Decodable words	help, helps, has, hits, Ben, Baker, bin, bad of, fun, fast, huff, puff, off, tells, Miss, mess
Common words	of, off, big
Common exception/irregular words ('tricky' words)	no, go, I

Developing vocabulary
Miss Baker, Slink, mess, fast

The Early Years Foundation Stage Framework**

Early Learning Goals (statutory requirement)		Assessment pointers in this story
ELG 01 Listening and attention	Children give their attention to what others say and respond appropriately, while engaged in another activity.	Check children listen and respond to your questions whilst they are reading the story.
ELG 02 Understanding	Children answer 'how' and 'why' questions about their experiences and in response to stories or events.	Check children understand how Ben tried to help Miss Baker and why he tripped up.
ELG 03 Speaking	Children use past, present and future forms accurately when talking about events that have happened or are to happen in the future.	Check children use the future tense when they discuss what might happen next.
ELG 09 Reading	They also read some common irregular words.	Check children are able to read common exception words listed.
ELG 10 Writing	Children use their phonic knowledge to write words in ways which match their spoken sounds.	Check children can use their phonic knowledge to write phonetically plausible attempts at longer words.

Oxford Reading Criterion Scale: Assessment Standard 1

No.	Criteria	Assessment pointers in this story
6	Is able to read some words from the YR high-frequency word list. (READ)	Check children can read the common words in the story.
10	Knows a wider range of GPCs and can sound and blend to read most CVC words (including words with double letters, e.g. bell, hiss). (READ)	Check the children recognize the focus GPCs and blend them to read the decodable words listed.
12	Can retell familiar stories with growing confidence. (R)	Check children can retell the story using the story map on p12.
14	Can recognize language patterns in stories, poems and other texts, e.g. repeated phrases, rhyme, alliteration. (A)	Check children can recognize Ben's repeated refrain 'Can I help?'

---

*For a full phonic breakdown, see the *Phonic and vocabulary overview* section in this handbook.

**Scottish Curriculum for Excellence/Foundation Phase Framework for Wales/Northern Ireland/Cambridge Primary English and International curricula correlation can be found online at: www.oxfordowl.co.uk

Before reading

Practise reading the common exception words listed.

- Key skills:
  - Look at the front and back cover illustrations. Read the title. Ask children who they think Ben is going to help in this story. **(Predicting, retrieve)**
  - Ask children where the story is taking place. What clues can they find in the pictures to support this? **(Previewing the text)**
  - Look at p2. Introduce the children to Miss Baker. Can they think what job she has in the school? (Dinner lady.) **(Predicting)**
  - Show children the word *mess*. Check children understand what the word means. Ask children to tell you about a time when they made a mess. **(Exploring new vocabulary, activating prior knowledge)**
- Strategy check:
  - Ask children to write the focus GPCs in the splats on the splat mat (PCM 30). Hold up a selection of the decodable words from the story. Ask children to blend to read the word, racing to splat the matching focus GPC on their mat. For example, they splat *ff* after reading the word *off*. **(Word reading)**

During reading

- Key skills:
  - Pause on p2. Tell children: *I like the way the author tells us that 'Ben can run as fast as a truck'. It helps me to get a picture in my head of how fast Ben can run as I know trucks can move very fast.* **(Visualising)**
  - Look at the words written in italics: *huff puff*. Ask children why the author has written these words next to Ben. **(Inferring, making connections)**
  - Pause on p6. Ben is being very helpful. Ask children if there are any clues to suggest that something is going to go wrong? **(Predicting)**
  - Pause on p8. Ask children how they would you feel if they were Miss Baker/Slink/ Ben? Encourage the children to share their ideas using their 'Feelings fan' (PCM 28). **(Empathizing)**

After reading

- Return to the text. Check if there were any words that the children found difficult to read. Clarify any errors if necessary. **(Word reading)**
- Key skills:
  - Turn to p12. Encourage the children to take turns with their talk partner to retell what is happening saying only one sentence for each picture. **(Summarizing)**
  - Ask children who was feeling happy when the pot of cod was dropped. Slink. **(Recall and retrieve)**
  - Reread p11. Ask children why Ben decided not to use his super speed this time. **(Deducing)**
  - Ask children to make a picture in their heads of Ben running at super speed. Can they imagine what else might move as fast as Ben? **(Visualizing, making connections)**.

Other things to do

- Writing activities
  - Miss Baker needs some warning signs for the kitchen to alert people to things that could be dangerous (hazards). Encourage the children to use their own drawings and writing to create some signs.
- Speaking, listening and drama
  - Do a Hero Academy kitchen role play with appropriate props. Ask children to make up their own stories based on events that might happen in the Hero Academy kitchen.
- Cross-curricular links
  - Involve the children in solving story-related problems requiring them to sort, match and count plates and cups and share out the sandwiches. **(Mathematics – numbers)**

Jin Lifts Off

Story summary

Mr Trainer is testing Jin's flying skills. Jin wants to pass the test so follows the directions quickly. He doesn't notice that he disturbs Slink's nap so Slink gets his own back!

Additional resources: Photocopiable master (PCM) 27: Thought bubble; story action words written on A4 card displayed with phoneme buttons.

Phonics and vocabulary checker*

Phonics	
Focus GPCs	j, v, w, x
Decodable words	Jin, just, vet, seven, will, twists, well, next, six, box
Common words	will
Common exception/irregular words ('tricky' words)	n/a

Developing vocabulary
Mr Trainer, Slink, pass, ducks, dips, twists, spins

The Early Years Foundation Stage Framework**

Early Learning Goals (statutory requirement)		Assessment pointers in this story
ELG 01 Listening and attention	Children listen to stories, accurately anticipating key events and respond to what they hear with relevant comments, questions or actions.	Check children can describe their favourite part of the story and comment on their friends' choices.
ELG 02 Understanding	Children follow instructions involving several ideas or actions.	Check children can follow simple directions as they move around the obstacle course test.
ELG 03 Speaking	Children develop their own narratives and explanations by connecting ideas or events.	Check children can explain what Slink might be thinking at different points in the story.
ELG 09 Reading	Children demonstrate understanding when talking with others about what they have read.	Check children can describe what Jin did in his test and decide why Slink gets him back.
ELG 10 Writing	Children use their phonic knowledge to write words in ways which match their spoken sounds.	Check children are matching spoken sounds to graphemes as they make signs for the obstacle course.

Oxford Reading Criterion Scale: Assessment Standard 1

No.	Criteria	Assessment pointers in this story
6	Is able to read some words from the YR high-frequency word list. (READ)	Check children can find and read the common words listed.
7	Can state simple likes/dislikes about familiar texts. (E)	Check children can talk about which parts of the story they liked and disliked.
11	Can point to a full stop in text. (READ)	Check children can point to the full stops in the main text and in the speech bubbles.
12	Can retell familiar stories with growing confidence. (R)	Check children can retell the story using the story map on p16.

*For a full phonic breakdown, see the *Phonic and vocabulary overview* section in this handbook.
**Scottish Curriculum for Excellence/Foundation Phase Framework for Wales/Northern Ireland/Cambridge Primary English and International curricula correlation can be found online at: www.oxfordowl.co.uk

Before reading

- Key skills:
  - ○ Look at the front and back cover. Read the title and blurb together. Reinforce that a 'test' can check how good you are at something. **(Exploring new vocabulary)**
  - ○ Turn to p3. Talk about what kind of test Jin might have to pass. Encourage the children to look briefly through the book for any clues. **(Previewing the text, predicting)**
  - ○ Ask children if they have met Jin before in any other stories. What is his superpower? **(Activating prior knowledge, making connections)**
- Strategy check:
  - ○ Tell children there are lots of action words in the story. Play a game of 'Jin says ...' to check that they understand each action. Use the action words from the story written with phoneme buttons on A4 card for them to read (spin/twist/duck/dip). **(Word reading, exploring new vocabulary)**

During reading

- Key skills:
  - ○ Encourage the children to look carefully for Slink on each page as they are reading and remember what he is doing.
  - ○ Pause on p6. Return to the predictions children made before reading. Did they make a good prediction? **(Recall, making connections)**
  - ○ Praise children 'in the moment' as they recognize the focus GPCs and blend to read each word on the run in the continuous text.
  - ○ Pause on p8. Ask children to tell their talk partner what Jin has done so far in his test. **(Summarizing, recall and retrieve)**
  - ○ Pause after reading Slink's thought bubble on p9. Ask children why Slink is thinking 'get the vet'. **(Inferring)**
  - ○ Pause after reading p12 and p13. Can children explain why Jin is looking so pleased? **(Deducing)**

After reading

- Return to the text. Check if there were any words that the children found difficult to read. Clarify any errors if necessary. **(Word reading)**
- Key skills:
  - ○ Ask children to talk about how they felt about the story, what their favourite part was, and share their reasons. **(Personal response)**
  - ○ Revisit the pages where Slink was featured and ask children to use their 'Thought bubble' (PCM 27) to suggest verbally what Slink might be thinking. **(Inferring)**
  - ○ Return to p10. Ask children how Slink got back to the box before Jin. **(Deducing)**
  - ○ Mr Trainer used a timer to measure how long Jin took to complete the test. Ask children to tell you why they thought Jin was fast/slow. **(Inferring)**
  - ○ Ask children why Slink decides to get Jin back at the end of the story. **(Recall and retrieve, activating prior knowledge)**

Other things to do

- Writing activities
  - ○ Encourage children to make signs to label their obstacle courses (see below) using the action words from the story to describe how to move around the course.
- Speaking, listening and drama
  - ○ Use construction kits and character puppets to recreate the obstacle course test. In pairs, take turns to give each other directions using the action words from the story.
- Cross-curricular links
  - ○ Help the children to set up their own obstacle courses in the outdoor area using small P.E. equipment. Explore using simple timers/stop watches to measure how long their friends take to complete the test. **(Physical Development – moving and handling; Mathematics – shape, space and measures)**

Will the Reds Win?

Story summary

Jin, Pip and Ben play a game of rounders with their friends. They use their superpowers to help the red team win the game.

Additional resources: Photocopiable master (PCM) 25: Speech bubble; PCM 29: Super spotter, populated with the focus GPCs one in each box.

Phonics and vocabulary checker*

Phonics	
Focus GPCs	j, v, w, x
Decodable words	Jin, jogs, jets, vest, vests, seven, will, win, next, six
Common words	will
Common exception/irregular words ('tricky' words)	n/a

Developing vocabulary
fast, jets

The Early Years Foundation Stage Framework**

Early Learning Goals (statutory requirement)		Assessment pointers in this story
ELG 01 Listening and attention	Children give their attention to what others say and respond appropriately, while engaged in another activity.	Check children are able to listen and pay attention to others as they take turns to sequence and summarize the story.
ELG 02 Understanding	Children answer 'how' and 'why' questions about their experiences and in response to stories or events.	Check children understand why Ben scores the most runs and how Jin catches the ball.
ELG 03 Speaking	Children use past, present and future forms accurately when talking about events that have happened or are to happen in the future.	Check children use the future tense when they are predicting who will win the game.
ELG 09 Reading	Children use phonic knowledge to decode regular words and read them aloud accurately.	Check children can locate and read the decodable words listed.
ELG 10 Writing	Children write simple sentences which can be read by themselves and others. Some words are spelt correctly and others are phonetically plausible.	Check children are able to write a simple sentence to describe their favourite part of the story.

Oxford Reading Criterion Scale: Assessment Standard 1

No.	Criteria	Assessment pointers in this story
3	When prompted, can use illustrations to support talk about what is happening in a text and to predict what might happen next. (D)	Check children understand the game being played and ask them to predict what some of the rules might be for 'super' rounders.
6	Is able to read some words from the YR high-frequency word list. (READ)	Check children can locate and read the common words listed.
10	Knows a wider range of GPCs and can sound and blend to read most CVC words (including words with double letters, e.g. bell, hiss). (READ)	Check the children can locate and read the decodable words listed.
12	Can retell familiar stories with growing confidence. (R)	Check children can retell the story using the story map on p16.

---

*For a full phonic breakdown, see the *Phonic and vocabulary overview* section in this handbook.

**Scottish Curriculum for Excellence/Foundation Phase Framework for Wales/Northern Ireland/Cambridge Primary English and International curricula correlation can be found online at: www.oxfordowl.co.uk

Before reading

- Key skills:
  - Look at the front and back cover and read the title and blurb together. Ask children what they think this story might be about. **(Predicting, making connections)**
  - Note the question mark in the title and explain that this punctuation tells us that this sentence is a question. Model how you would change your voice when asking a question and invite the children to practise. **(Fluency)**
  - Turn to p2. Look at the characters in the story. Ask children if they think the characters will use their superpowers to help them win the game. **(Predicting)**
  - Ask children if they have ever played rounders or a similar game. Look briefly at the illustrations to give them some clues about how to play and encourage them to make connections with their personal experiences. **(Activating prior knowledge, previewing the text)**
- Strategy check:
  - Use PCM 29 ('Super spotter'). Check the children can recall the focus GPCs written on their spotter. Challenge them to look for these GPCs in words as they are reading. They can tick or tally mark how many words they find or write the word in the correct GPC box. **(Word reading)**

During reading

- Key skills:
  - One of the teams is called the *red vests*, but we don't know the name of the other team. Ask children to see if they can find this out as they read the story. **(Recall and retrieve)**
  - Pause on p5. Help children to decode the words 'fast' and 'seven'. How many runs did Ben get? Explain that a run is scored by running around the four bases on the field. **(Exploring new vocabulary)**
  - Pause after reading p6–7. Jin is looking in the sky for the ball that Pip has hit. Ask children what information suggests that Pip is good at batting. **(Inferring, recall and retrieve)**
  - Pause on p11. Ask children why Pip has a shocked expression. **(Inferring)**
  - Ask children to continue reading independently to the end of the story.

After reading

- Return to the text. Check if there were any words that the children found difficult to read or understand. Clarify any errors if necessary. **(Word reading)**
- Key skills:
  - Which team did children want to win the game? Do they think it was fair that Ben and Jin used their superpowers to help their team win? **(Personal response)**
  - Return to p 9. Ask children to share ideas with their talk partner about what Jin might be thinking and saying. Use the 'Speech bubble' (PCM 25) to practise saying their ideas aloud in role as Jin. **(Empathizing, inferring)**
  - Turn to p15. Ask children to explain why they think Jin's feelings have changed at the end of the story. **(Deducing, empathizing)**

Other things to do

- Writing activities
  - Invite children to draw a picture of their favourite part of the story and encourage them to add a simple sentence to describe what is happening.
- Speaking, listening and drama
  - Using the story map on p16, ask children to pick one picture and orally rehearse a simple sentence to summarize what is happening. **(Summarizing)**
- Cross-curricular links
  - Practise playing bat and ball games in the outdoor area. Encourage the children to use simple tally marks to record the scores/count runs. **(Physical development – moving and handling; Mathematics – numbers)**

The Zipbot

Story summary

Ben invents a Zipbot machine and Pip tests it out. The Zipbot goes wrong so Ben has to use his super-speed to catch up and stop it.

Additional resources: Photocopiable master (PCM) 15: Machine name generator; PCM 30: Splat mat, populated with the focus graphemes.

Phonics and vocabulary checker*

Phonics	
Focus GPCs	y, z, zz, qu
Decodable words	yet, yes, Zipbot, zigzags, buzz, quick, quack
Common words	n/a
Common exception/irregular words ('tricky' words)	he, she

Developing vocabulary
zigzags, grass, skids

The Early Years Foundation Stage Framework**

Early Learning Goals (statutory requirement)		Assessment pointers in this story
ELG 01 Listening and attention	Children give their attention to what others say and respond appropriately, while engaged in another activity.	Check children listen carefully to others as they plan and make their Zipbot models.
ELG 02 Understanding	Children follow instructions involving several ideas or actions.	Check children can follow simple instructions to draw a picture of the Zipbot described.
ELG 03 Speaking	Children express themselves effectively, showing awareness of listeners' needs.	Check children can express their views to the group about the safety of the Zipbot.
ELG 09 Reading	Children use phonic knowledge to decode regular words and read them aloud accurately.	Check children can locate and read the decodable words listed.
	Children read and understand simple sentences.	Check children can read the simple sentences on pages.
ELG 10 Writing	Children use their phonic knowledge to write words in ways which match their spoken sounds.	Check children can add labels to their Zipbot designs using their phonic knowledge to write simple VC and CVC words.

Oxford Reading Criterion Scale: Assessment Standard 1

No.	Criteria	Assessment pointers in this story
7	Can state simple likes/dislikes about familiar texts. (E)	Check children can talk about which parts of the story they liked and disliked.
11	Can point to a full stop in text. (READ)	Check children can point to full stops in the main text and in speech bubbles.
12	Can retell familiar stories with growing confidence. (R)	Check children can retell the story using the story map on p16.
18	With support, can find information to help answer simple, literal questions. (R)	Check children can answer questions about what happened first, next etc.

*For a full phonic breakdown, see the *Phonic and vocabulary overview* section in this handbook.
**Scottish Curriculum for Excellence/Foundation Phase Framework for Wales/Northern Ireland/Cambridge Primary English and International curricula correlation can be found online at: www.oxfordowl.co.uk

Before reading

- Key skills:
    - Pay a quick game of phoneme splat. Call out the focus phonemes one at a time. The children splat the matching grapheme on their 'Splat mat' (PCM 30).
    - Look at the front cover and read the title together. Model how to read *zip* and then *bot* before blending the whole word Zipbot. Remind them that chopping the word into syllables (chunks) makes it easier to read. **(Word reading, strategy check)**
    - Turn to p4. Ben gives Pip a helmet. Ask children why it's important for her to wear one in the Zipbot. Can they tell you about a time when they have worn a helmet? **(Previewing the text, activating prior knowledge)**
    - Locate and read the word *zig zag* on p6. Explain that it describes the way the Zipbot is moving. Can they use their finger to trace a zigzag pattern in the air? **(Exploring new vocabulary)**
- Strategy check:
    - Tell children that this book contains two new tricky words '*he*' and '*she*'. Remind them that they need to try to read the word on sight. Explain that the author has used '*he*' and '*she*' instead of saying the boy/Ben or the girl/Pip all of the time. If appropriate mention that these words have a special name: pronouns. **(Word reading)**

During reading

- Key skills:
    - Ask children what they think the Zipbot machine can do. **(Predicting)**
    - Pause on p6. The Zipbot is moving fast. Ask children what might happen next. **(Predicting, inferring)**
    - Praise children 'in the moment' as they recognize the focus GPCS and blend to read each word. Support and note children who have difficulties decoding words in isolation or to read simple sentences.
    - Pause on p8. Model how Pip might be feeling: *If I was Pip I would be feeling … because …* Ask children how they might feel if they were driving the Zipbot. **(Empathizing)**
    - Pause on p11. Ask children why Pip wants Ben's help quickly. What dangers can they spot? **(Recall and retrieve, inferring)**

After reading

- Return to the text. Check if there were any words that the children found difficult to read. Invite the children to show examples of the new tricky words that they found in the story. Clarify any errors if necessary.
- Key skills:
    - Ask children if they think it was safe for Pip to test the Zipbot. Encourage them to listen to each other's ideas and decide whether they agree or have a different idea. **(Personal response, deducing)**
    - Ask children to explain what caused the Zipbot to go out of control. **(Summarizing, recall and retrieve, inferring)**
    - Ask children to imagine they are Ben at the beginning of the story. What instructions should they give Pip to help her drive the Zipbot safely? **(Activating prior knowledge, making connections)**.

Other things to do

- Writing activities
    - Ask children to draw and label a design for a new Zipbot machine. Demonstrate how the children can use the 'machine name generator' on PCM 15 to create a name for their Zipbot.
- Speaking, listening and drama
    - Ask children to work in small groups to plan and make their own Zipbot machines using recycled materials. Challenge them to listen carefully to each other's ideas and make decisions together.
- Cross-curricular links
    - Set up an obstacle course and work in teams to direct a programmable/remote control toy from the start to the finish. **(Understanding the World – technology; Mathematics – shape, space and measures)**

Pip's Mess

Story summary

Pip is experimenting with liquids in the lab when she trips and adds too much. Things start to go wrong and poor Slink gets a shock! Mrs Molten comes to the rescue.

Additional resources: Photocopiable master (PCM) 28: Feelings fan.

Phonics and vocabulary checker*

Phonics	
Focus GPCs	y, z, zz, qu
Decodable words	yuck, yells, zap, zip, buzz, fizzes, liquid, quick
Common words	n/a
Common exception/irregular words ('tricky' words)	he, she

Developing vocabulary
Mrs Molten, Slink, fizzes

The Early Years Foundation Stage Framework**

Early Learning Goals (statutory requirement)		Assessment pointers in this story
ELG 01 Listening and attention	Children listen to stories, accurately anticipating key events and respond to what they hear with relevant comments, questions or actions.	Check children can summarize what has happened so far in the story (up to p4).
ELG 02 Understanding	Children answer 'how' and 'why' questions about their experiences and in response to stories or events.	Check children understand why Pip uses her super strength to pick Ben up and how Mrs Molten stops the liquid.
ELG 03 Speaking	Children develop their own narratives and explanations by connecting ideas or events.	Check children can explain what happened to Slink when the liquid drops on him.
ELG 09 Reading	They also read some common irregular words.	Check children can read on sight the common exception words.
ELG 10 Writing	Children use their phonic knowledge to write words in ways which match their spoken sounds.	Check children are using their GPC knowledge to write a list of ingredients for their invisibility mixture.

Oxford Reading Criterion Scale: Assessment Standard 1

No.	Criteria	Assessment pointers in this story
7	Can state simple likes/dislikes about familiar texts. (E)	Check children can talk about which parts of the story they liked and disliked.
10	Knows a wider range of GPCs and can sound and blend to read most CVC words (including words with double letters, e.g. bell, hiss). (READ)	Check the children can locate and read the decodable words listed.
12	Can retell familiar stories with growing confidence. (R)	Check children can retell the story using the story map on p16.
18	With support, can find information to help answer simple, literal questions. (R)	Check children can talk about what happened first, next etc.

*For a full phonic breakdown, see the *Phonic and vocabulary overview* section in this handbook.
**Scottish Curriculum for Excellence/Foundation Phase Framework for Wales/Northern Ireland/Cambridge Primary English and International curricula correlation can be found online at: www.oxfordowl.co.uk

Before reading

- Key skills:
  - Look at the front and back cover and read the title and blurb. Ask children what they think Pip has done to make such a mess. Have they ever made a mess? **(Predicting, activating prior knowledge)**
  - Talk about where the story is set. Explain that *lab* is short for *laboratory*. Ask children what clues in the pictures help them to understand what they might learn about in a lab? **(Previewing the text)**
  - Turn to p4. Locate the word *liquid*, notice the 'qu' digraph. Ask children to name any liquids that they can think of. **(Exploring new vocabulary, activating prior knowledge)**
  - Look closely at the information on the whiteboard behind Mrs Molten on p4. Ask children what the information might be/be for. What might the mixture do? **(Inferring, predicting)**

During reading

- Key skills:
  - Turn to p3. Ask children why Pip is saying yuck when she is holding the mixture. **(Inferring)**
  - Pause on p4. Pip has made a mistake. Ask children to summarize what has happened so far. **(Summarizing)**
  - Praise children 'in the moment' as they recognize the focus GPCs and blend to read each word. Support and note children who have difficulties decoding words in isolation or reading simple sentences.
  - Pause on p7. Ask children what they think might happen next. **(Prediction)**
  - Pause on p12. Ask children why Mrs Molten pours the purple liquid on to Slink. **(Inferring)**
  - Ask children to continue reading independently to the end of the story.

After reading

- Return to the text. Check if there were any words that the children found difficult to read or understand. Clarify any errors if necessary. **(Word reading)**
- Key skills:
  - Return to p6. Ask children what happened to the mixture when Pip added lots of the yellow liquid. Can they recall a time when they have seen a liquid fizz? **(Activating prior knowledge, making connections, recall and retrieve)**
  - Ask children to think back to their predictions before reading. What did they think the mixture could do? Can they explain what happened to Slink? Introduce children to the words *invisible/disappear* to help with their explanations. **(Recall and retrieve, exploring new vocabulary)**
  - Return to p10. Ask children why Pip used her super-strength to pick Ben up. What do we know about the liquid Pip dropped that might help us to explain this? **(Deducing)**
  - At the end of the story it tells us that Slink is mad. Using the 'Feelings fan' (PCM 28) ask children to talk with their partners about how they would have felt if Pip had made them invisible. **(Empathizing)**

Other things to do

- Writing activities
  - Encourage the children to create their own invisibility mixture recipes. Challenge the children to use their own drawings and writing to make a list of ingredients they would include.
- Speaking, listening and drama
  - Ask children to consider if they would like to have the superpower to become invisible. Help scribe a list of the advantages and disadvantages of being invisible.
- Cross-curricular links
  - Safely explore mixing baking soda with vinegar and washing up liquid to make fizzy potions. **(Expressive arts and design – exploring media and materials; Understanding the World – the world)**

Slink's Snack

Story summary

Slink is feeling peckish so he sneaks into the kitchen for a midnight snack. He gets a big shock when Miss Baker catches him eating tomorrow's lunch!

Additional resources: Photocopiable master (PCM) 26: Magnifying glass; 2 minute sand timer; sticky notes/flashcards of focus GPCs.

Phonics and vocabulary checker*

Phonics	
Focus GPCs	ch, sh, th, ng, nk
Decodable words	checks, chicken, chips, lunch, such, peckish, fresh, fish, dish, mash, shock, crash, mash, then, this, that, bath, clang, long, Slink, drink, sink
Common words	that, this, then
Common exception/irregular words ('tricky' words)	me

Developing vocabulary
Miss, Baker, peckish, mash

The Early Years Foundation Stage Framework**

Early Learning Goals (statutory requirement)		Assessment pointers in this story
ELG 01 Listening and attention	Children give their attention to what others say and respond appropriately, while engaged in another activity.	Check children listen to their friend's opinions about Miss Baker being cross and offer their own ideas.
ELG 02 Understanding	Children answer 'how' and 'why' questions about their experiences and in response to stories or events.	Check children understand why Miss Baker was cross with Slink and how Slink ended up covered in food.
ELG 03 Speaking	Children express themselves effectively, showing awareness of listeners' needs.	Check children can add appropriate expression when they read 'bad cat'.
ELG 09 Reading	Children use phonic knowledge to decode regular words and read them aloud accurately.	Check children locate the focus digraphs and read the decodable words in the story.
ELG 10 Writing	Children write simple sentences which can be read by themselves and others. Some words are spelt correctly and others are phonetically plausible.	Check children make phonetically plausible attempts at words like sorry/ forgive.

Oxford Reading Criterion Scale: Assessment Standard 1

No.	Criteria	Assessment pointers in this story
6	Is able to read some words from the YR high-frequency word list. (READ)	Check children can read the common words listed.
8	Can talk about the main points/key events in a text, e.g. main story setting, events, principle character. (R)	Check children can talk about what happened first, next etc.
15	Can read words with consonant diagraphs: ch, sh, th, ng. (READ)	Check children can read the decodable words listed.
21	Is beginning to make predictions based on titles, text, blurb and/or illustrations. (D)	Check children can talk about the title and the blurb and predict what Slink might be up to in the story.

*For a full phonic breakdown, see the *Phonic and vocabulary overview* section in this handbook.
**Scottish Curriculum for Excellence/Foundation Phase Framework for Wales/Northern Ireland/Cambridge Primary English and International curricula correlation can be found online at: www.oxfordowl.co.uk

Before reading

- Key skills:
  - Look at the front and back cover. Read the title and blurb. Check the children's understanding of what a snack is and encourage them to share examples of what they might eat for a snack. **(Activating prior knowledge, exploring new vocabulary)**
  - Turn to p3. Ask children what time of day this story takes place. What makes them think that? **(Predicting, previewing the text)**
  - Turn to p6. Ask children where Slink has gone to get a snack. **(Previewing the text)**
  - Turn to p11 and locate the tricky word *me*. Make a link to the previous tricky words: *he, she*. The grapheme 'e' represents /ee/ not /e/ in all of these words.
- Strategy check:
  - Ask children to take it in turns to turn over a sticky note/flashcard for each focus GPC and say the phoneme that matches the grapheme they see. Keep their cards for later. Then remind them of digraphs: write the word *fish* on a whiteboard and draw a phoneme button under each phoneme. Remind children in this word the 's' and 'h' are making the /sh/ sound not /s/ /h/.

During reading

- Key skills:
  - Ask children to be phoneme detectives. As they read, ask them to use their 'Magnifying glass' (PCM 26) to locate words in the story that contain the GPC on the sticky note/flashcard they were given.
  - Pause on p4. Ask children why Slink is looking so happy in this picture. **(Recall and retrieve, inferring, empathizing)**
  - Praise children 'in the moment' as they recognize the focus GPCs and blend to read each word. Support and note children who have difficulties decoding words in isolation or reading simple sentences. **(Word reading)**
  - Pause on p10. With their talk partners, give children two minutes against the timer to list the snacks Slink got in order from first to last. Can they use the connectives *first, next, then*? **(Summarizing)**
  - Pause on p13. Draw children's attention to the exclamation mark after 'Bad cat'. Ask children how Miss Baker is feeling? Try reading this with an angry voice. **(Fluency)**
  - Ask children to continue reading independently to the end of the story.

After reading

- Return to the text. Check if there were any words that the children found difficult to read/understand. Clarify any errors if necessary.
- Key skills:
  - Return p12. Ask children to create a picture in their head of Slink alone in the dark kitchen in the middle of the night. Suddenly he sees a dark shadow. What could Slink be thinking? **(Visualizing, deducing)**
  - Ask children if they think it was right that Miss Baker was cross with Slink. Ask children to discuss with their talk partner. **(Recall and retrieve, personal response)**
  - Look back through the story and ask children to try to find at least 3 things that have gone wrong for Slink. **(Empathizing, deducing)**

Other things to do

- Writing activities
  - Ask children to write a 'sorry' note to Miss Baker from Slink. What might Slink say? Can they include the tricky words: *I* and *me* in their message?
- Speaking, listening and drama
  - Discuss children's favourite snack foods. Encourage them to ask questions and share their opinions in response to to what their friends say.
- Cross-curricular links
  - Encourage the children to experiment with creating 'kitchen sound effects'. Provide a selection of suspended metal pots/pans, and metal kitchen utensils for the children to explore. **(Expressive Arts and Design – exploring media and materials)**

Fix That Bell!

Story summary

The school lunch bell won't stop ringing. Ben tries to help Magnus fix the bell, but the springs ping out over the lunch hall floor. Can Magnus and Ben save the day?

Additional resources: Photo of a toolbox and tools or role play DIY toolbox.

Phonics and vocabulary checker*

Phonics	
Focus GPCs	ch, sh, th, ng, nk
Decodable words	lunch, chips, much, sandwich, peckish, dash, fish, rushes, with, then, think, this, that, thanks, rings, ring, springs, ping, drink
Common words	that, this, then, them, with
Common exception/irregular words ('tricky' words)	we, me, be

Developing vocabulary
Mrs Butterworth, peckish, dash, pass, pulls, springs (metal coils)

The Early Years Foundation Stage Framework**

Early Learning Goals (statutory requirement)		Assessment pointers in this story
ELG 01 Listening and attention	Children give their attention to what others say and respond appropriately, while engaged in another activity.	Check children listen carefully as they discuss what tools Magnus might have used to fix the bell.
ELG 02 Understanding	Children answer 'how' and 'why' questions about their experiences and in response to stories or events.	Check children understand why Ben didn't get to eat his lunch and how the heroes felt when the lunch bell wouldn't stop ringing.
ELG 03 Speaking	Children develop their own narratives and explanations by connecting ideas or events.	Check children can connect events from the story as they explain to Magnus what has happened.
ELG 09 Reading	Children read and understand simple sentences.	Check children are beginning to read simple sentences more fluently.
	They also read some common irregular words.	Check children can locate and read the new common exception words listed.
ELG 10 Writing	Children use their phonic knowledge to write words in ways which match their spoken sounds.	Check children have used their knowledge of the focus GPCs to label food/drink items on their menus.

Oxford Reading Criterion Scale: Assessment Standard 1

No.	Criteria	Assessment pointers in this story
6	Is able to read some words from the YR high-frequency word list. (READ)	Check children can read the common words listed.
10	Knows a wider range of GPCs and can sound and blend to read most CVC words (including words with double letters, e.g. bell, hiss). (READ)	Check children are confident in reading familiar words with double letters, e.g. *bell*.
15	Can read words with consonant diagraphs: ch, sh, th, ng. (READ)	Check children recognize the digraphs and read the decodable words listed.
21	Is beginning to make predictions based on titles, text, blurb and/or illustrations. (D)	Check children can make predictions about the story based on the blurb.

*For a full phonic breakdown, see the *Phonic and vocabulary overview* section in this handbook.
**Scottish Curriculum for Excellence/Foundation Phase Framework for Wales/Northern Ireland/Cambridge Primary English and International curricula correlation can be found online at: www.oxfordowl.co.uk

Before reading

Practise reading the common exception words listed.

- Key skills:
  - Read the title and look at the cover illustration. Ask children what *to fix* means. **(Exploring new vocabulary)**
  - Talk about a time you tried to fix something. Then ask children if they have ever tried to fix something. Remind children that we can make connections with our experiences to help us make predictions and understand the story. **(Activating prior knowledge)**
  - Ask children what they think might happen in this story. **(Predicting)**
  - Look at p6–7. Ask children where this story is taking place. **(Previewing the text)**
  - Write the word *sandwich* on a mini whiteboard. Ask children to spot any digraphs. Remind children to break the word into syllables (chunks) sand/wich; blend to read each syllable separately and then put the word together. **(Word reading)**
- Strategy check:
  - Read the sentence on p2 in a robotic voice and then reread it adding appropriate expression. Ask children which sounds better. Ask children to practise reading with expression. **(Fluency)**

During reading

- Key skills:
  - Pause on p7. Ask children what will happen next. Share their ideas with a talk partner. **(Predicting)**
  - Praise children who notice the two digraphs in *think* (p7) and *thanks* (p15) before they blend to read them, and support children who struggle by writing these words on a mini whiteboard and adding sound buttons to help them recognize the digraphs before they blend the words. **(Word reading)**
  - Pause on p8. Ask children to help Ben explain to Magnus what has happened. **(Summarizing)**
  - Praise children whose reading sounds interesting/not robotic and give them 'in the moment' specific praise about the strategies they have used. **(Fluency)**

After reading

- Return to the text. Check if there were any words that the children found difficult to read/understand. Clarify any errors and model strategies if necessary.
- Key skills:
  - Ask children why Ben didn't get to eat his fish and chips. How would they feel if they were Ben? **(Inferring, empathizing)**
  - Return to p9. Ask children why Magnus asked Ben to pass him the box. Look at an image of a toolkit and tools or bring along a role play toolkit. What tools do they think Magnus used to fix the bell? **(Deducing, making connections)**
  - Still on p9, ask children what Ben told Magnus as he was rushing back to the lunch hall. **(Recall and retrieve, deducing)**
  - Ask children to reread their favourite part of the story with a talk partner. Remind them to try not to sound like a robot with long pauses between each word! **(Personal response, fluency)**

Other things to do

- Writing activities
  - Ask children to write a menu so the heroes know what they can choose to eat for lunch. Look at some simple menus. Invite children to draw and label at least four different foods and drinks using their phonic knowledge.
- Speaking, listening and drama
  - Ben and Magnus persevered when the springs sprung out of the bell. Ask children to talk about a time when they persevered and didn't give up when something went wrong. Model as appropriate.
- Cross-curricular links
  - The lunch bell makes a loud sound. Investigate the sounds made by a range of percussion instruments that ring and compare loud and quiet sounds. **(Understanding the World – technology)**

It is Freezing

Story summary

The heroes enjoy playing together in the snow. Pip uses her super-strength to help her friends make a snow sculpture and Slink gets a big surprise!

Additional resources: Photocopiable master (PCM) 30: Splat mat populated with the focus GPCs; memory box with a photo of children playing in the snow or a note that says 'think back to a snowy day'.

Phonics and vocabulary checker*

Phonics	
Focus GPCs	ai, ee, igh, oa
Decodable words	wait, trail, tail, freezing, needs, three, see, sighs, light, high, coat, loads, groans, coal, cloak
Common words	see, too
Common exception/irregular words ('tricky' words)	her

Developing vocabulary
fast, push groans

The Early Years Foundation Stage Framework**

Early Learning Goals (statutory requirement)		Assessment pointers in this story
ELG 01 Listening and attention	Children listen to stories, accurately anticipating key events and respond to what they hear with relevant comments, questions or actions.	Check children can respond with appropriate comments as they predict what type of snow sculpture it is.
ELG 02 Understanding	Children follow instructions involving several ideas or actions.	Check children can follow instructions to make the snow cloud dough.
ELG 03 Speaking	Children use past, present and future forms accurately when talking about events that have happened or are to happen in the future.	Check children are using the past tense when they discuss their experiences of playing in the snow.
ELG 09 Reading	They also read some common irregular words.	Check children can read the common exception words listed.
	Children demonstrate understanding when talking with others about what they have read.	Check children understand the problems Ben and Jin faced and how Pip used her super strength to solve this.
ELG 10 Writing	Children use their phonic knowledge to write words in ways which match their spoken sounds.	Check children can recall the focus GPCs as they write a list of materials for their snow sculptures.

Oxford Reading Criterion Scale: Assessment Standard 1

No.	Criteria	Assessment pointers in this story
18	With support, can find information to help answer simple, literal questions. (R)	Check children can find clues about what the weather is like in the story.
19	Can read words with some vowel digraphs e.g. /ai/ /ee/ /igh/ /oa/. (READ)	Check children can read the decodable words that include the focus GPCs listed.
20	Can talk about main points or key events in a simple text. (R)	Check children can retell the story using the story map on p16.
23	Knows the function of full stops when reading and shows this in their reading aloud. (READ)	Check children can demonstrate use of full stops when reading aloud the main text and the speech and thought bubbles.

*For a full phonic breakdown, see the *Phonic and vocabulary overview* section in this handbook.
**Scottish Curriculum for Excellence/Foundation Phase Framework for Wales/Northern Ireland/Cambridge Primary English and International curricula correlation can be found online at: www.oxfordowl.co.uk

Before reading

- Key skills:
    - Look at the front and back cover and read the title. Ask children what they think the weather is going to be like in this story. Why? **(Predicting)**
    - Introduce the children to the memory box and share the photo or note. Reflect on a time when you had fun in the snow. Invite children to join in with their own experiences. **(Activating prior knowledge)**
    - Look briefly through the book. Are there any clues in the picture to support their predictions about the weather? **(Previewing the text, making connections)**
    - Check children understand the meaning of the word *freezing*. Suggest some foods that they can think of that feel freezing cold. **(Exploring new vocabulary)**
- Strategy check:
    - Give each child a 'Splat mat' (PCM 30) with the focus GPCs written on it. Check their recall of the new focus GPCs encouraging them to splat the correct grapheme as you say each phoneme.
    - Talk about 'igh'. Explain that there are three letters representing the phoneme /igh/ and that we call this a trigraph. Practise reading high and sigh. Orally segment/blend a selection of the listed decodable words as the children listen carefully for one of the focus GPCs and then splat the corresponding grapheme on their mat.

During reading

- Key skills:
    - Remind children to look out for exclamation marks (p3, p4, p8, and p14) as they are reading and note which children remember to use appropriate emotion as they are reading. **(Fluency)**
    - Pause on p3. The teacher calls out to Pip to wait. Ask children why she tells Pip to get her coat. **(Inferring)**
    - Praise children 'in the moment' as they recognize the focus GPCs and blend to read each word. Support and note children who have difficulties decoding words in isolation or reading simple sentences. **(Word reading)**
    - Pause on p9. Ask children to explain to their talk partners the problems Ben and Jin have had so far in the story. How were their problems solved? **(Summarizing)**
    - Pause on p11. Ask children what type of snow sculpture they think the characters are making. **(Predicting, making connections)**

After reading

- Return to the text. Check if there were any words that the children found difficult to read/understand. Clarify any errors and model strategies if necessary.
- Key skills:
    - Ask children if they think the heroes were enjoying themselves in the snow. Get them to look back through the story and find clues that support their ideas. **(Empathizing, deducing)**
    - Slink does a lot of thinking in this book. Ask children how we know this. (Use of thought bubbles). Draw attention to the question marks (p9 and p12) and explain that these tell us that Slink is asking a question. Ask children to reread his thoughts adding expression. Model this for the children. **(Word reading, fluency)**
    - Ask children to describe their favourite part of the story and explain why. **(Personal response)**
    - Ask children what clues Pip and Jin gave Slink as they were making their snow sculpture. **(Recall and retrieve, deducing)**

Other things to do

- Writing activities
    - Discuss what the heroes used to decorate the snow sculpture. Ask children to write a list of materials that they might need to decorate their own snow sculptures.
- Speaking, listening and drama
    - Create a snow themed small world scene in a builder's tray using related story characters and props. Can they use the story map on p16 to retell the story?
- Cross-curricular links
    - Make a snow cloud dough recipe using a cup of plain flour and a cup of cooking oil mixed together. Add white/silver glitter if desired. Get them to make their own snow sculptures. **(Expressive Arts and Design – exploring media and materials; Understanding the World – the world)**

Win the Cup!

Story summary

The heroes enter a dance competition, but the judges aren't impressed with their moves. It looks like no one will win the cup until the final contestant takes to the floor.

Additional resources: Photocopiable master (PCM) 25: Speech bubble; PCM 28: Feelings fan; PCM 29: Super spotter, populated with listed tricky words.

Phonics and vocabulary checker*

Phonics	
Focus GPCs	ai, ee, igh, oa
Decodable words	tail complain, train, see, feet, need, keep, agree
Common words	see, too
Common exception/irregular words ('tricky' words)	was, her

Developing vocabulary
boasts, fast, complain

The Early Years Foundation Stage Framework**

Early Learning Goals (statutory requirement)		Assessment pointers in this story
ELG 01 Listening and attention	Children listen to stories, accurately anticipating key events and respond to what they hear with relevant comments, questions or actions.	Check children can generate questions for Slink about his dancing and winning the cup.
ELG 02 Understanding	Children answer 'how' and 'why' questions about their experiences and in response to stories or events.	Check children understand why Ben, Jin and Pip did not win and how Slink was feeling when he won.
ELG 03 Speaking	Children express themselves effectively, showing awareness of listeners' needs.	Check children can express their opinions on Ben, Jin and Pip's dancing.
ELG 09 Reading	Children read and understand simple sentences.	Check children understand to change their voice when reading sentences punctuated with speech marks.
ELG 10 Writing	Children use their phonic knowledge to write words in ways which match their spoken sounds.	Check children can use the focus GPCs as they write labels for Slink's dance moves: spins, tail twists, feet taps, high kick.

Oxford Reading Criterion Scale: Assessment Standard 1

No.	Criteria	Assessment pointers in this story
17	Without prompting, uses words and illustrations together to gain meaning from a text. (R/D)	Check children can explain why Ben, Jin and Pip do not win the cup.
20	Can read words with some vowel digraphs e.g. /ai/ /ee/ /igh/ /oa/. (READ)	Check children can read the decodable words that include the focus GPCs listed.
21	Is beginning to make predictions based on titles, text, blurb and/or illustrations. (D)	Check children can make predictions about what the cup/trophy is for.
23	Knows the function of full stops when reading and shows this in their reading aloud. (READ)	Check children can demonstrate the use of full stops when reading aloud the main text and the speech bubbles.

*For a full phonic breakdown, see the *Phonic and vocabulary overview* section in this handbook.
**Scottish Curriculum for Excellence/Foundation Phase Framework for Wales/Northern Ireland/Cambridge Primary English and International curricula correlation can be found online at: www.oxfordowl.co.uk

Before reading

Practise reading the decodable words listed. Check that children understand their meaning.

- Key skills:
  - Look at the front and back covers and read the title/blurb together. Reinforce that *cup* is used as another word for trophy. **(Exploring vocabulary)**
  - Ask children what the cup/trophy is for. Are there any clues on the cover/title page? **(Predicting)**
  - Turn to p4–5. Do these illustrations confirm children's predictions? Did they predict it was a dancing competition? Point to the judging panel and clarify their job. **(Previewing the text)**
  - Tell children this reminds you of a programme on TV where people perform dance routines. Invite children to talk about similar programmes they have seen or tell the group about their own experiences of being in a competition. **(Activating prior knowledge)**
- Strategy check:
  - Hold up the 'Speech bubble' (PCM 25) and reinforce what the reader has to do when he/she sees them in a story. In this story the author has used speech bubbles, but they have also used speech marks (draw on a whiteboard) to tell the reader when a character is speaking. Explain that the words inside the speech marks are what the character says so they need to change their voice to sound like them when they read it. Model and invite the children to practise this. **(Fluency, word reading)**

During reading

- Key skills:
  - Look at p3 together. Help the children to read *tonight* on a mini whiteboard. Mask *night* using a sticky note and read the tricky word *to,* and then say the GPCs and blend to read *night* noticing the trigraph /igh/ in the middle of the word. **(Word reading)**
  - Provide specific 'in the moment' praise when children blend to read words containing the focus GPCs including the polysyllabic word *complain*. Praise and note which children pay attention to the speech marks and change their voices.
  - Read p4–9. Ask children to pretend to be one of the judges and share their opinion of Ben, Jin and Pip's dancing with their talk partner. **(Recall and retrieve, summarizing)**
  - Ask children who they think is the best dancer so far. Can they explain their choice? **(Inferring)**

After reading

- Return to the text. Give the children the 'Super spotter' (PCM 29) populated with the tricky words from the story (one per box). Can they read each word and then go back through the book to locate them? They should add a tick/tally mark every time they find an example. **(Word reading)**
- Key skills:
  - Return to p10. Mrs Molten said that they might need to keep the cup. Why did she think this? **(Deducing)**
  - Ask children to imagine that they are a character at the end of the story (not Slink). Use their 'Feelings fan' (PCM 28) to help them decide how they were feeling when they lost the competition using information from the story to explain. **(Empathizing)**
  - Ask children to recall the dance moves Slink included in his winning dance. **(Recall and retrieve)**

Other things to do

- Writing activities
  - Ask children to select a character from the story and write at least one simple sentence to explain why they didn't win.
- Speaking, listening and drama
  - Invite children to think of questions that they would like to ask Slink about his dancing skills/winning the competition. (Provide simple recording device/digital microphone to record the interview).
- Cross-curricular links
  - Set up a 'dance off' competition in the outdoor area. Invite the children to choose their own music and create their own dance. **(Physical Development – moving and handling; Expressive Arts and Design – being imaginative)**

Turnip is Missing

Story summary

Magnus is worried: his pet rat, Turnip, is missing! Ben uses his super-speed to help search for him. He spots Turnip in the garden and devises a plan to catch him.

Additional resources: Photocopiable master (PCM) 21: Two syllable words; PCM 26: Magnifying glass; PCM 28: Feelings fan; decodable words containing the grapheme 'oo' written on to sticky notes; flashcards for the focus GPCs.

Phonics and vocabulary checker*

Phonics	
Focus GPCs	oo (look), oo (zooms), ar, or, ur
Decodable words	looking, book, look, looks, room, scoots, soon, food, scoops, darts, garden, for, thorns, sweetcorn, Turnip, bursts, fur, curls, turns
Common words	look, for
Common exception/irregular words ('tricky' words)	my, you

Developing vocabulary
fast, darts, scoots, scoops

The Early Years Foundation Stage Framework**

Early Learning Goals (statutory requirement)		Assessment pointers in this story
ELG 01 Listening and attention	Children listen to stories, accurately anticipating key events and respond to what they hear with relevant comments, questions or actions.	Check children listen carefully to their peers and remember the events in sequence in the memory game.
ELG 02 Understanding	Children follow instructions involving several ideas or actions.	Check children are able to follow their talk partner's instructions to locate the rat.
ELG 03 Speaking	Children develop their own narratives and explanations by connecting ideas or events.	Check children can suggest new ideas for Turnip's next adventures.
ELG 09 Reading	Children read and understand simple sentences.	Check children read and understand Ben's plan on p9.
ELG 10 Writing	Children use their phonic knowledge to write words in ways which match their spoken sounds.	Check children have segmented and used the focus GPCs to write their lists of action words from the story.

Oxford Reading Criterion Scale: Assessment Standard 1

No.	Criteria	Assessment pointers in this story
17	Without prompting, uses words and illustrations together to gain meaning from a text. (R/D)	Check children can predict who Turnip might be.
19	Can read words with some vowel digraphs e.g. /ai/ /ee/ /igh/ /oa/ /oo/. (READ)	Check children can read the decodable words listed choosing the correct pronunciation for the 'oo' grapheme.
20	Can talk about main points or key events in a simple text. (R)	Check children can retell the story using the story map on p16.
22	Can read almost all the YR high-frequency words. (READ)	Check children can read the common words listed.

---

*For a full phonic breakdown, see the *Phonic and vocabulary overview* section in this handbook.
**Scottish Curriculum for Excellence/Foundation Phase Framework for Wales/Northern Ireland/Cambridge Primary English and International curricula correlation can be found online at: www.oxfordowl.co.uk

Before reading

Practise reading the common exception words listed.

- Key skills:
  - ○ Look at the front cover and read the title. Ask children who Turnip might be and what clues give this away. Read the blurb. Does this give us any more information? **(Predicting, inferring)**
  - ○ Check that children understand the concept of something going 'missing'. **(Exploring new vocabulary)**
  - ○ Talk about a time when you had something go missing. Invite children to share their own experiences. **(Activating prior knowledge, making connections)**
  - ○ Review the focus GPCs 'ar', 'or' and 'ur' written on sticky notes. Challenge the children to look for these whilst they are reading.
- Strategy check:
  - ○ Show the grapheme 'oo' and explain that in some words it makes the phoneme /oo/ as in *look* but in other words it makes the phoneme /oo/ as in *zoom*. Make two columns on a whiteboard using these words as headers. Invite the children to pick up a 'oo' word sticky note from the pile, practise reading the word deciding which phoneme the 'oo' grapheme represents and add it to the correct column. **(Word reading)**

During reading

- Key skills:
  - ○ Challenge children to use their 'Magnifying glass' (PCM 26) to help them spot Turnip on every page.
  - ○ Get children to imagine they are Ben. Where might they look for Turnip? **(Predicting)**
  - ○ Explain that good readers will reread the word/sentence if it doesn't make sense. Demonstrate this by rereading a word/sentence that a child has made an error on. **(Fluency)**
  - ○ Pause on p7. Ask children why they think Turnip decides to run away from Ben. **(Inferring)**
  - ○ Pause on p9. Ask children to tell their talk partners about Ben's plan to catch Turnip. Do they think it will work? **(Summarizing)**
  - ○ Ask children to continue reading to the end of the story. What has happened? Practise reading the text in Magnus' speech bubble to show how he is feeling when Turnip escapes again! Remind children to look at the punctuation (? and !) to help you decide on the expression to use. **(Fluency, empathizing)**

After reading

- Return to the text. Check if there were any words that the children found difficult to read or understand. Clarify any errors if necessary.
- Key skills:
  - ○ Ask children to talk about the part of the story they liked the most and why. Encourage them to respond to what their friends say. **(Personal response)**
  - ○ The author has used a selection of different action words to describe how Ben and Turnip move, e.g. *darts* (p4). Ask children to write down as many action words as they can find.
  - ○ Ask children to think about Magnus' feelings at different points in the story. Encourage them to use their feelings fan (PCM 28) to help decide if his feelings change and the causes of this. **(Empathizing)**
  - ○ Return to p14. Ask children if they think it was sensible for Turnip to be in Magnus' pocket. Ask them to think back to what they know about keeping small pets. What advice would they give Magnus to stop Turnip escaping again? **(Deducing, making connections)**

Other things to do

- Writing activities
  - ○ Ask children to complete PCM 21 practising blending to read and then write two syllable words.
- Speaking, listening and drama
  - ○ Look at p15. It looks like Turnip is off on a new adventure. Play a memory game: the adult starts the game by saying, *Turnip goes off on a new adventure. He creeps through the science lab.* The next child has to repeat what you have said and add their own idea for where Turnip goes.
- Cross-curricular links
  - ○ Set up a small world scene of Hero Academy with character props for Ben and Turnip. The children take turns to hide Turnip using positional language to describe to their talk partner where to find him. **(Mathematical Development – shape, space and measures)**

Zoom Food

Story summary

Jin wants to be as fast as Ben, so he asks Mrs Butterworth to help him make some zoom food. However, Jin eats too much and can't stop. Who will come to his rescue?

Additional resources: Photocopiable master (PCM) 22: Mrs Butterworth's cook book.

Phonics and vocabulary checker*

Phonics	
Focus GPCs	*oo* (look), *oo* (zooms), ar, or, ur
Decodable words	book, books, look, looks, cook, good, zoom, zooms, food, beetroot, spoon, too, shoots, dart, stars, for, popcorn, turnip, burst, slurps, turn, turns
Common words	look, for
Common exception/irregular words ('tricky' words)	my, you

Developing vocabulary
Mrs Butterworth, zoom, fast, beetroot, burst of speed, past, pull

The Early Years Foundation Stage Framework**

Early Learning Goals (statutory requirement)		Assessment pointers in this story
ELG 01 Listening and attention	Children listen attentively in a range of situations.	Check children listen carefully as they play the 'In my zoom food' game.
		Check children can hear and say words that rhyme with *zoom*.
ELG 02 Understanding	Children answer 'how' and 'why' questions about their experiences and in response to stories or events.	Check children understand why Mrs Butterworth was concerned when Jin flew off and how she helped him.
ELG 03 Speaking	Children develop their own narratives and explanations by connecting ideas or events.	Check children can explain why Jin went to see Mrs Butterworth connecting information from the story to help them.
ELG 09 Reading	Children read and understand simple sentences.	Check children are checking for sense when they read and self-correcting any substitutions/omissions.
	They also read some common irregular words.	Check children read the common exception words listed.
ELG 10 Writing	Children use their phonic knowledge to write words in ways which match their spoken sounds.	Check children are using their knowledge of the focus GPCs as they write a list of ingredients.

Oxford Reading Criterion Scale: Assessment Standard 1

No.	Criteria	Assessment pointers in this story
19	Can read words with some vowel digraphs e.g. /ai/ /ee/ /igh/ /oa/ /oo/. (READ)	Check children can blend to read the decodable words listed choosing the correct pronunciation for the 'oo' grapheme.
20	Can talk about main points or key events in a simple text. (R)	Check children can retell the story using the story map on p16.
22	Can read almost all the YR high-frequency words. (READ)	Check children can read the common words in the story.
23	Knows the function of full stops when reading and shows this in their reading aloud. (READ)	Check children can read with expression, correctly emphasizing the full stop.

*For a full phonic breakdown, see the *Phonic and vocabulary overview* section in this handbook.
**Scottish Curriculum for Excellence/Foundation Phase Framework for Wales/Northern Ireland/Cambridge Primary English and International curricula correlation can be found online at: www.oxfordowl.co.uk

Before reading

Practise reading the common exception words listed.

- Key skills:
  - ○ Look at the front cover and read the title together. Praise children for pronouncing the /oo/ correctly in *zoom* and *food*. Check children understand the meaning of the word *zoom*. **(Word reading, exploring new vocabulary)**
  - ○ Tell children you've never heard of 'zoom food'. Ask them to imagine what it tastes like and why Jin might be eating it. **(Predicting, activating prior knowledge)**
  - ○ Look at p 2 and the characters in this story. Ask children what this tells us about Jin and comment on the author's comparison with flying like a rocket. Is that high? How do you know? **(Previewing the text)**
  - ○ Turn to p5. What could the books on Mrs Butterworth's kitchen shelf be about? Discuss what information they might find in them and link to their own experiences of looking at recipes when cooking at home. **(Activating prior knowledge)**
- Strategy check:
  - ○ Remind children of the focus GPCs and review strategies for reading words with the grapheme 'oo' in them.

During reading

- Key skills:
  - ○ Pause on p 6. Ask children to explain to their talk partner why Jin visits Mrs Butterworth. **(Recall and retrieve, summarizing)**
  - ○ Pause on p7. Ask children to explain the word *ingredients* and how it relates to this page.
  - ○ Pause on p10. Mrs Butterworth looks concerned. Ask children what she is worried about. **(Inferring)**
  - ○ Praise children 'in the moment' as they recognize the focus GPCs and blend to read each word. Support and note children who have difficulties decoding words in isolation or reading simple sentences. **(Word reading)**
  - ○ Pause on p11. Ask children what they think might happen next. **(Predicting)**
  - ○ Ask children to continue reading independently to the end of the story.

After reading

- Return to the text. Check if there were any words that the children found difficult to read or understand. Clarify any errors and model strategies if necessary.
- Key skills:
  - ○ Turn to p12. Read this page aloud to them. Ask them to follow the text and listen carefully for any errors. Read robotically using your finger and substitute 'turn' for 'tum' and 'stars' for 'stairs'. Ask the children to discuss the way you read it and if they noticed any errors. Have they got any top tips for you that a good reader uses? **(Fluency)**
  - ○ Challenge children to explain how Mrs Butterworth and Ben helped Jin to stop. Check they understand the purpose of a crash bag. **(Recall and retrieve)**
  - ○ Jin ate too much zoom food. What tips would they give Jin to make sure the problem doesn't happen again? **(Deducing, recall and retrieve)**
  - ○ Ask children how they think Jin is feeling when he can't stop. **(Empathizing)**
  - ○ Ask children to find their favourite part of the story and reread it to the group. Ask them to read it with expression so that their friends will be interested to listen. **(Fluency, personal response)**

Other things to do

- Writing activities
  - ○ Ask children to complete PCM 22 ('Mrs Butterworth's cook book').
- Speaking, listening and drama
  - ○ Play a memory game: *In my zoom food I put* ... The first child starts off by saying: "In my zoom food I put a fish." The next child repeats what the first child has said and adds an extra ingredient.
- Cross-curricular links
  - ○ Invite children to explore non-fiction books or look at child-friendly websites to find out about keeping healthy and the importance of a healthy diet. Can they make some posters to display in the classroom? **(Physical Development – health and self-care)**

Stuck in the Storm

Story summary

Pip, Jin and Slink get caught out in a storm when a tree is struck by lightning and blocks the school entrance. Pip uses her super-strength to clear the way.

Additional resources: Photocopiable master (PCM) 25: Speech bubble; PCM 26: Magnifying glass; PCM 29: Super spotter, populated with the focus GPCs; two minute sand timer.

Phonics and vocabulary checker*

Phonics	
Focus GPCs	ow (cow), oi, ear, (near), ure, air, er
Decodable words	power, frowns, meow, towels, soil, avoid, hear, clear, appear, sure, air, hair, thunder, better
Common words	down, now
Common exception/irregular words ('tricky' words)	they, all, are

Developing vocabulary
thunder, avoid, fast, skid/skidding, appears, soaking

The Early Years Foundation Stage Framework**

Early Learning Goals (statutory requirement)		Assessment pointers in this story
ELG 01 Listening and attention	Children listen to stories, accurately anticipating key events and respond to what they hear with relevant comments, questions or actions.	Check children can listen carefully to the description of the storm and paint a picture in their head of what they can see/hear.
ELG 02 Understanding	Children answer 'how' and 'why' questions about their experiences and in response to stories or events.	Check children can summarize why Pip and Jin were stuck in the storm and how Pip solved the problem.
ELG 03 Speaking	Children use past, present and future forms accurately when talking about events that have happened or are to happen in the future.	Check children are using the present tense when they describe what they can see/hear in the storm.
ELG 09 Reading	Children use phonic knowledge to decode regular words and read them aloud accurately.	Check children can blend to read the decodable words listed, recognizing the focus GPCs.
ELG 10 Writing	Children use their phonic knowledge to write words in ways which match their spoken sounds.	Check children write the focus GPCs as they make a list of things they might hear and see in the storm.

Oxford Reading Criterion Scale: Assessment Standard 1

No.	Criteria	Assessment pointers in this story
7	Can state simple likes/dislikes about familiar texts. (E)	Check children can talk about which parts of the story they liked and disliked.
22	Can read almost all the YR high-frequency words. (READ)	Check children can read the common and common exception words in the story.
23	Knows the function of full stops when reading and shows this in their reading aloud. (READ)	Check children can read with expression, correctly emphasizing the full stop.
24	Can read most common CVC words automatically, without the need for sounding and blending. (READ)	Check children are checking for sense when they read and self-correcting any substitutions/omissions.

*For a full phonic breakdown, see the *Phonic and vocabulary overview* section in this handbook.

**Scottish Curriculum for Excellence/Foundation Phase Framework for Wales/Northern Ireland/Cambridge Primary English and International curricula correlation can be found online at: www.oxfordowl.co.uk

Before reading

Practise reading the common exception words listed.

- Key skills:
  - Look at the front cover and read the title. Ask children why the characters might be stuck in the storm. **(Predicting)**
  - Talk about a time when you got caught in a storm; what happened? Ask children to tell you about a storm they have seen or been out in. What was it like? How did they feel? **(Activating prior knowledge)**
  - Turn to p4 and p7. Check the children's understanding of the words *lightning* and *thunder*. Reinforce reading the word *lightning* by chunking into syllables light/ning, blending the phonemes in each syllable and then putting the word back together. **(Previewing the text, exploring vocabulary, word reading)**
- Strategy check:
  - Give children a copy of PCM 29 populated with the focus GPCs. Ask them which are digraphs/trigraphs. Give the children two minutes against the timer to go through the book looking for words containing the focus GPCs. Note these on their spotter grid.

During reading

- Key skills:
  - The author has used speech marks in this book. Review their purpose. Ask children to notice when speech marks are used, using their 'Speech bubble' (PCM 25) to practise changing their voice based on how the character would say it.
  - Pause on p4. Ask children why Jin is covering his ears and Slink looks worried. **(Empathizing)**
  - Praise children 'in the moment' as they recognize the focus GPCs and blend to read each word. Support and note children who have difficulties decoding words in isolation or reading simple sentences. **(Word reading)**
  - Pause on p5. Check that children understand the word *avoid*. What was Pip keen to avoid? **(Exploring new vocabulary, recall and retrieve)**
  - Pause on p8. Ask children what they would do if they were Pip and Jin. How could they solve the problem? **(Personal response, making connections)**
  - Pause on p13. Ask children why Pip and Jin are doing a 'high five'. **(Inferring)**
  - Ask children to continue reading independently to the end of the story.

After reading

- Return to the text. Check if there were any words that the children found difficult to read or understand. Clarify any errors if necessary.
- Key skills:
  - Ask children to explain to their talk partner what the problem was and how the heroes solved it. **(Summarizing, recall and retrieve)**
  - Ask children if they think it is safe to go out in a storm. Share their ideas as a group and use information from the story to support their decision. **(Personal response, deducing)**
  - Invite children to close their eyes as they listen to you reread the first part of the story (pages 4–8) which describe the storm. Encourage them to paint a picture in their mind of the storm and imagine that they are there with Pip and Jin. How would they feel? Write a list/discuss the things that they would see and hear. **(Visualizing, empathizing)**.

Other things to do

- Writing activities
  - Look at non-fiction books or watch a child-friendly clips of a storm to find out more information. Can they make an information leaflet about storms?
- Speaking, listening and drama
  - Work in small groups to reread p4–6 of the story thinking about the sound effects they could add to make it more realistic. Experiment with using a range of percussion instruments to add sound effects for the storm.
- Cross-curricular links
  - Invite the children to close their eyes and listen to a storm-themed soundtrack/music, e.g. Vivaldi, *Storm*. What pictures can they see in their head? Challenge them to work collaboratively to paint a largescale 'stormy day' picture. **(Expressive Arts and Design – exploring media and materials)**

The Fizzing Mixture

Story summary

Mrs Molten has set the class a test. Things start to go wrong when Ben doesn't follow the instructions for his mixture. Mrs Molten ends up floating in the air.

Additional resources: Photocopiable master (PCM) 24: Match sentences to the pictures; PCM 27: Thought bubble; PCM 30: Splat mat, populated with listed common exception words.

Phonics and vocabulary checker*

Phonics	
Focus GPCs	ow (cow), oi, ear, (near), ure, air, er
Decodable words	powder, powders, frowns, how, down, now, spoil, boil, clear, dear, near, sure, mixture, cure, air, stairs, her, darker, ladder
Common words	down, now
Common exception/irregular words ('tricky' words)	they, all, are

Developing vocabulary
Mrs Molten, fast, mixture, frowns, splashes, darts-up, pass

The Early Years Foundation Stage Framework**

Early Learning Goals (statutory requirement)		Assessment pointers in this story
ELG 01 Listening and attention	Children listen attentively in a range of situations.	Check children listen carefully as they share ideas about whether Ben should have past Mrs Molten's test.
ELG 02 Understanding	Children follow instructions involving several ideas or actions.	Check children can follow instructions to blend to read polysyllabic words.
ELG 03 Speaking	Children develop their own narratives and explanations by connecting ideas or events.	Check children can summarize why Mrs Molten is floating near the roof, listing the events that lead to this.
ELG 09 Reading	Children demonstrate understanding when talking with others about what they have read.	Check children demonstrate their understanding about what happened to Ben's fizzing mixture.
ELG 10 Writing	Children write simple sentences which can be read by themselves and others. Some words are spelt correctly and others are phonetically plausible.	Check children are using the focus GPCs to segment and write a simple thank you message.

Oxford Reading Criterion Scale: Assessment Standard 1

No.	Criteria	Assessment pointers in this story
20	Can talk about main points or key events in a simple text. (R)	Check children can retell the story using the story map on p16.
21	Is beginning to make predictions based on titles, text, blurb and/or illustrations. (D)	Check children can predict what might happen in the story from the title and the blurb.
22	Can read almost all the YR high-frequency words. (READ)	Check children can read the common and common exception words in the story.
24	Can read most common CVC words automatically, without the need for sounding and blending. (READ)	Check children are checking for sense when they read and self-correcting any substitutions/omissions.

---

*For a full phonic breakdown, see the *Phonic and vocabulary overview* section in this handbook.
**Scottish Curriculum for Excellence/Foundation Phase Framework for Wales/Northern Ireland/Cambridge Primary English and International curricula correlation can be found online at: www.oxfordowl.co.uk

Before reading

- Key skills:
  - Look at the front cover and read the title, demonstrating how to decode the word *fizzing* by chunking it into syllables. Repeat with the word *mixture*. **(Word reading)**
  - Ask children what they think Ben's mixture might do. **(Predicting)**
  - Look at p2 and p3. Ask children which characters are in the story and where it is set. **(Previewing the text)**
  - Check children's understanding of the challenge words in the story. Clarify the meaning of each by asking children to put them into a sentence. **(Exploring new vocabulary)**
- Strategy check:
  - Review the common exception words listed. Play *tricky word splat* using a populated version of PCM 30. Encourage the children to finger splat the corresponding tricky word as you call it out. You could add some other, previously covered, common exception words too.

During reading

- Key skills:
  - Ask children to read p3 independently.
  - Ask children who they think will pass Mrs Molten's test. What does she ask them to do? **(Predicting, recall and retrieve)**
  - Pause on p5. Pip and Mrs Molten look shocked. Ask children why they think they might feel concerned. **(Inferring, empathizing)**
  - Praise children 'in the moment' as they recognize the focus GPCs and blend to read each word including chunking and blending polysyllabic words. Support and note children who have difficulties decoding words in isolation or reading simple sentences. **(Word reading)**
  - Read p6–9. Ask children why Mrs Molten is floating near the roof. Get them to summarize for their talk partner what has happened since Ben added too much powder to his mixture. **(Summarizing)**
  - Ask children who they think Ben will get to help Mrs Molten and how will they get her down. **(Predicting)**

After reading

- Return to the text. Check if there were any words that the children found difficult to read or understand. Clarify any errors and model strategies if necessary.
- Key skills:
  - Ask children why the heroes are all wearing goggles in the lab. **(Inferring, making connections)**
  - Tell children that you're not sure that Ben should have passed the fizzing mixture test because he didn't listen to Mrs Molten's instructions. Ask children who agrees/disagrees. **(Deducing)**
  - Ask children what feature the author has used to tell us what Ben is thinking (thought bubbles). Challenge them to use their thought bubble outline (PCM 27) to model what Mrs Molten is thinking on p5, p9, p13 and p15. **(Empathizing, inferring)**

Other things to do

- Writing activities
  - Ben would like to write a thank you message to Magnus for helping him. Involve the group in planning and orally rehearsing what they want to say before writing their message.
- Speaking, listening and drama
  - Enlarge and cut up the picture sequence cards from PCM 24. Prerecord each story sentence on a talk button. Ask children to sequence the picture cards in the correct order. Listen to each talk button and match it to the correct part of the story. Use the story map on p16 to check they have sequenced the story correctly.
- Cross-curricular links
  - Provide a selection of child-safe powders (baking powder/flour) in a small tray and liquids (water/vinegar both in small squeezy bottles or pipettes) with a range of graded receptacles. Challenge the children to investigate combining different mixtures to see if they can make a mixture that fizzes. **(Understanding the World – the world; Mathematics – shape, space and measures)**

Assessing progress

The Early Years Foundation Stage (EYFS) specifies statutory requirements for areas of learning and development, which must inform adults' planning of activities and experiences for children. Teachers make summative judgements about the level of progress children have made at the end of the EYFS (in YR) against the criteria in the Early Learning Goals.

Ongoing formative assessment is a fundamental part of the learning and development process in Reception/Primary 1 and contributes to making those summative Early Years Foundation Stage Profile (EYFSP) judgements. Assessing children to identify next steps in learning for each child is a key undertaking for all Early Years practitioners. Cumulative observations of children in a range of provision are required – independent, adult-supported and adult-led learning experiences. This is acutely so for assessment for the areas of Communication and Language and of Literacy.

However, assessment does not exist in a vacuum!

Teachers must ensure that their specific and continuous provision allows and supports children to demonstrate what they *'know and can do'* in their emerging reading and writing skills in order that it can be robustly assessed. Therefore conducting periodic checks of the enabling learning environment for literacy is time well spent. The DfE publication *Development Matters in the Early Years Foundation Stage* provides a useful initial starting point for auditing teaching practice and provision.

The areas of learning and development requirements:

Communication and Language: development involves giving children opportunities to experience a rich language environment; to develop their confidence and skills in expressing themselves; and to speak and listen in a range of situations

Literacy: development involves *encouraging children to link sounds and letters and to begin to read and write. Children must be given access to a wide range of reading materials (books, poems, and other written materials) to ignite their interest.*[1]

Practitioners should note the learning which a child demonstrates spontaneously, independently and consistently in a range of contexts.[2]

Assessment and progress tracking were believed to be only valuable if used effectively to support learning and development, identify children requiring additional support, and feed into curriculum planning.[3]

---

[1] *Statutory Framework for the Early Years Foundation Stage,* Department for Education, © Crown copyright 2017.

[2] *Early Years Foundation Stage Profile, 2017 Handbook,* Department for Education, © Crown copyright 2016.

[3] Callanan M., Anderson M., Haywood S., Hudson R. and Speight S., *Study of Early Education and Development: Good Practice in Early Education,* Department for Education, © NatCen Social Research, 2017.

Development Matters in the Early Years Foundation Stage[1]

	Positive Relationships (what adults could do)	Enabling Environments (what adults could provide)
30–50 Months	• Focus on meaningful print such as a child's name, words on a cereal packet or a book title, in order to discuss similarities and differences between symbols. • Help children to understand what a word is by using names and labels and by pointing out words in the environment and in books. • Provide dual language books and read them with all children, to raise awareness of different scripts. Try to match dual language books to languages spoken by families in the setting. • Remember not all languages have written forms and not all families are literate either in English, or in a different home language. • Discuss with children the characters in books being read. • Encourage them to predict outcomes, to think of alternative endings and to compare plots and the feelings of characters with their own experiences. • Plan to include home language and bilingual story sessions by involving qualified bilingual adults, as well as enlisting the help of parents.	• Provide some simple poetry, song, fiction and non-fiction books. • Provide fact and fiction books in all areas, e.g. construction area as well as the book area. • Provide books containing photographs of the children that can be read by adults and that children can begin to 'read' by themselves. • Add child-made books and adult-scribed stories to the book area and use these for sharing stories with others. • Create an environment rich in print where children can learn about words, e.g. using names, signs, posters. • When children can see the text, e.g. using big books, model the language of print, such as *letter, word, page, beginning, end, first, last, middle.* • Introduce children to books and other materials that provide information or instructions. • Carry out activities using instructions, such as reading a recipe to make a cake. • Ensure access to stories for all children by using a range of visual cues and story props.
40–60 Months	• Discuss and model ways of finding out information from non-fiction texts. • Provide story sacks and boxes and make them with the children for use in the setting and at home. • Encourage children to recall words they see frequently, such as their own and friends' names. • Model oral blending of sounds to make words in everyday contexts, e.g. *'Can you get your h-a-t hat?'* • Play games like word letter bingo to develop children's phoneme-grapheme correspondence. • Model to children how simple words can be segmented into sounds and blended together to make words. • Support and scaffold individual children's reading as opportunities arise.	• Encourage children to add to their first-hand experience of the world through the use of books, other texts and information, and information and communication technology (ICT). • Help children to identify the main events in a story and to enact stories, as the basis for further imaginative play. • Provide story boards and props which support children to talk about a story's characters and sequence of events. • When children are ready (usually, but not always, by the age of five) provide regular systematic synthetic phonics sessions. These should be multisensory in order to capture their interests, sustain motivation and reinforce learning. • Demonstrate using phonics as the prime approach to decode words while children can see the text, e.g. using big books. • Provide varied texts and encourage children to use all their skills including their phonic knowledge to decode words. • Provide some simple texts which children can decode to give them confidence and to practise their developing skills.

[1] Early Education, *Development Matters in the Early Years Foundation Stage,* © Crown copyright 2012.

Assessment to inform next steps in learning to read and write needs to distinguish the complex nature of learning to read and the interdependency of all aspects of literacy. The Early Learning Goal for Reading illustrates the importance of decoding words and also understanding what has been read. In addition, observations should be made of the child's attitudes to reading and their engagement with a variety of reading experiences. All three are needed to be a reader. Schools' observation and assessment processes need to reflect this too.

> *Assessment should not entail prolonged breaks from interaction with children, nor require excessive paperwork. Paperwork should be limited to that which is absolutely necessary to promote children's successful learning and development.*[1]

Phonic skills and knowledge

Teachers should be observing for evidence that children are applying their phonic skills and knowledge in the discrete phonics session, in independent and adult-supported reading and writing across the areas of learning, both indoors and outdoors. The format provides an opportunity for teachers to periodically record their formative assessments to build up a cumulative picture of what pupils know and can do. It has three aspects: GPC knowledge, phonics skills, and reading and spelling of common exception words.

> **The Early Learning Goals: Specific areas: Literacy:**
>
> *Reading: children read and understand simple sentences. They use phonics knowledge to decode regular words and read them aloud accurately. They also read some common irregular words. They demonstrate understanding when talking with others about what they have read.*[2]

The *Phonics skills and knowledge progress check* charts and the *Assessment of reading comprehension skills and behaviours* on the following pages, and the *Reading journey record* on page 24, offer a simple and effective way of recording what children know and can do and identifying next steps in learning. They can be adapted for use with individuals or groups of children.

[1/2] *Statutory Framework for the Early Years Foundation Stage*, Department for Education, © Crown copyright 2017.

Phonic skills and knowledge progress check

Oxford Level 1, Lilac A Book Band: Letters and Sounds Phase 1[1]

On entering Reception/Primary 1, *Listen, observe and note* how well children:

- Can continue a spoken rhyming string
- Are able to distinguish speech sounds (phonemes)
- Can articulate speech sounds clearly

- Are developing the skill to orally blend and segment phonemes in words (e.g. cat, wig, coat, sheep) and remember them in the order in which they occur
- Can identify the number of phonemes in a given word

Note: children should be assessed orally. There is no requirement for children to use or recognize graphemes at this phase.

Name:

Listen, observe and note how well child can …	Example	Observed (insert dot or tick and date)	Notes and comments
Recognize rhyming words	"In his pot, Ben has a pin and a tin, a hat and a cat and a mat."		
Continue a spoken rhyming string	"Jin knows a word that rhymes with *rock*. You put it on your foot and the word is … *sock*"		
Distinguish speech sounds (phonemes)	"What has Pip got in her school bag today? A b-b-b-bun, a b-b-b-bug, a b-b-b-bed, a b-b-b-bucket."		
Articulate phonemes	Children can isolate initial phoneme from the rest of the word e.g. recognizes that *Pip, pit, pet, pat* begin with /p/		
Orally blend phonemes in CVC words in the order in which they occur	Play the game Cross the River. Call out the name of an object in sound talk. Say the chant "Slink, can we cross your deep blue river?" Child has to blend the phonemes of the object to make the word and cross the river.		
Orally segment phonemes in CVC words in the order in which they occur	Sound talk games … Tell Slink in sound talk, e.g. "Tell Slink … that we drink out of a /m/ /u/ /g/ - mug; that we eat our dinner with a /f/ /or/ /k/ - fork."		
Identify the number of phonemes in a given word	Phoneme fingers – match each phoneme to a raised finger one-by-one and count, e.g. How many sounds can we hear in the word *bin* … b-i-n … *three*. How many sounds can we hear in the word *vest* … v-e-s-t … *four*.		

[1] *Letters and Sounds: Principles and Practice of High Quality Phonics*, Department for Children, Schools and Families © Crown copyright 2007, & *Getting to Grips with Assessing Pupil Progress*, Department for Children, Schools and Families © Crown Copyright 2009.

Phonic skills and knowledge progress check

Oxford Levels 1–1+, Lilac (B)–Pink (D) Book Bands: Letters and Sounds Phase 2[1]

Children secure at Phase 2 should:

Give the sound when shown any Phase 2 GPC; find any Phase 2 grapheme when given the sound.

Blend and segment VC and CVC words containing Phase 2 GPCs.

Read the common exception words: to, the, no, go, I.

Name:

Insert dot or tick and date when child demonstrates knowledge or skill

Phase 2	Set 1			Set 2				Set 3				Set 4				Set 5					Notes and comments
	s	a	t	p	m	i	d	n	g	o	c	k	ck	e	u	r	h	b	f	l	ll	ss	
Gives sound																							
Identifies grapheme																							
Blends to read all through the word	e.g. tap, pat			e.g. Pip, pit, tips, it, in, is, sit, mad, and				e.g. got, gap, spots, not, on, cod, can, cat, kit, skids				e.g. kick, tuck, pick, get, pet, runs, up, gust, stuck, rat, runs, rock				e.g. help, has, hits, bin, bad, bed, of, fun, off, puff, tells, ill miss, mess					
Reads common exceptionwords												to		the			no		go		I			

[1] Letters and Sounds: Principles and Practice of High Quality Phonics, Department for Children, Schools and Families © Crown copyright 2007, & Getting to Grips with Assessing Pupil Progress, Department for Children, Schools and Families © Crown Copyright 2009.

Phonic skills and knowledge progress check

Oxford Levels 2–3, Red–Yellow Book Bands: Letters and Sounds Phase 3[1]

Children secure at Phase 3 should:

Give the sound when shown any Phase 2 or 3 GPC; find any Phase 2 or 3 grapheme when given the sound.

Blend and segment VC and CVC words using Phase 2 and 3 GPCs.

Read the common exception words: *to, the, no, go, I, he, she, me, we, be, was, her, my, you, they, all, are*; spell common irregular words: *the, to, I, know, go.*

Name:

Insert dot or tick and date when child demonstrates knowledge or skill

Phase 3	Set 6				Set 7																							Notes and comments
	j	v	w	x	y	z	zz	qu	ch	sh	th	ng	ai	ee	igh	oa	oo	oo	ar	or	ur	ow	oi	ear	air	ure	er	
Gives sound																												
Identifies grapheme																												
Blends to read all through the word	e.g just, jogs, jet, vet, vest, twist, will, well, next, box, six				e.g. yes, yell, yet, zip, zap, buzz, quick, quack				e.g chips, much, such, shock, mash, then, this, ring, spring				e.g. wait, tail, trail, see, feet, need, high, might, float, boast				e.g. zoom, spoon, too, book, look, cook, darts, star, for, corn, burst, turns, slurps					e.g. powder, frown, how, boil, spoil, soil, clear, appear, near, air, hair, stair, sure, cure, better, power, darker							
Reads common exception words				he	she	me	we	be	was	her	my	you	they													all	are	

Child should also be able to spell common exception words from Phase 2: *to, the, no, go, I.*

---

[1] *Letters and Sounds: Principles and Practice of High Quality Phonics*, Department for Children, Schools and Families © Crown Copyright 2009. *& Getting to Grips with Assessing Pupil Progress*, Department for Children, Schools and Families © Crown copyright 2007.

Assessment of reading comprehension skills and behaviours[1]

*Children read and understand simple sentences. They use phonics knowledge to decode regular words and read them aloud accurately. **They also read common irregular words. They demonstrate understanding when talking with others about what they have read.*** ELG – reading

Reception/Primary 1

Name:

Skill	Behaviour (based on texts read by child and/or listened to)	Observed (insert dot or tick and date)	Notes and comments
Listening to and talking about reading	Listens to and joins in with poems and stories		
	Talks about stories, poems and information text		
Predicting	Joins in with repeated refrains and predicts key events and phrases		
	Makes simple predictions based on story content, illustrations and title		
	Suggests how a story might end		
Recall and sequencing	Recalls main events in sequence		
	Describes main story, settings, events and characters		
	Identifies main events/key points		
Awareness of story structure	Talks about themes, e.g. being kind, good vs evil		
	Beginning to be aware of the way stories are structured		
	Uses structure when retelling or re-enacting		
Responding to questions	Answers literal and retrieval questions about the text		
	Makes simple deductions with support		
Monitoring own understanding	Check/monitors own understanding while reading, e.g. stops reading and rereads word or sentence to check it makes sense		

This chart can be used to gather information, over time, about a child's developing comprehension.

[1] Criteria based on: Early Education, *Development Matters in the Early Years Foundation Stage* © Crown copyright 2012, & *Getting to Grips with Assessing Pupil Progress*, Department for Children, Schools and Families © Crown Copyright 2009.

HERO ACADEMY

Oxford assessment and levelling

Regular, systematic assessment of children's reading development is essential to the teaching process, helping review children's progress, and informing future teaching.

At the heart of Oxford Assessment and Levelling is the *Oxford Reading Criterion Scale* which describes the reading 'journey' that children make, breaking down children's reading development into small steps so that it is easy to identify the stage children have reached, and to work out what each child needs to do next. The *Oxford Reading Criterion Scale* is the result of many years' research into children's reading development by Ros Wilson, Sarah Threlkeld-Brown, schools and former Andrell Education Consultants.

The *Oxford Reading Criterion Scale* can be used termly to assess children's reading using an 'unseen' text at an appropriate level. Through hearing the child read and talking about the book, a teacher can observe the skills and strategies a child is using and can make a judgement about how secure each skill is. The 'score' that this assessment process generates will help you identify the Oxford Level a child is most comfortable reading at, and it will help you identify the precise next steps of learning for each child.

On the following pages, you will find the *Oxford Reading Criterion Scale* assessment charts for Pre-Reading Standard and Standard 1. Most children at Reception/Primary 1 should be working comfortably within these standards. Some, more able children, may reach Standard 2, which can be found in the *Hero Academy Teaching Handbook for Year 1/Primary 2*.

Assessing phonics

The *Oxford Reading Criterion Scale* includes many criteria that relate to children's phonic knowledge and skills but the underpinning assumption is that most schools will be using a systematic synthetic phonics programme to teach early reading. The *Oxford Reading Criterion Scale* does not duplicate this detailed phonic assessment process – instead, it offers you a flexible assessment tool that sits alongside the phonics assessment you are already doing, helping you to complete the picture you get of children's overall reading development. For detailed phonics tracking, you will find *Phonic skills and knowledge progress check* charts on pages 105–107 of this handbook.

The *Oxford Reading Criterion Scale* and other assessment and levelling systems

The chart below shows how the *Oxford Reading Criterion Scale* relates to Oxford Levels and Book Bands. The links between the *Oxford Reading Criterion Scale* and Book Bands are approximate and are given for general guidance only.

Year Group	Oxford Reading Criterion Scale Standard	Oxford Level	Book Band
Reception/P1	Pre-reading Standard	Level 1 or 1+	Lilac/Pink
	Standard 1: Developing	Levels 1+/2	Pink/Red
	Standard 1: Secure	Level 3	Yellow
	Standard 1: Advanced	Level 4	Light Blue
Year 1/P2	Standard 2: Developing	Levels 4/5	Light Blue/Green
	Standard 2: Secure	Level 6	Orange
	Standard 2: Advanced	Levels 7/8	Turquoise/Purple
Year 2/P3	Standard 3: Developing	Levels 7/8	Turquoise/Purple
	Standard 3: Secure	Levels 9/10	Gold/White
	Standard 3: Advanced	Level 11/12	Lime/Lime +

How to use the *Oxford Reading Criterion Scale* for assessment

Termly summative assessment

Summative assessments can be carried out in small groups or with individual children.

- Organize children into small groups of no more than four and, using your knowledge of the children's reading, select the *Oxford Reading Criterion Scale* Standard which is most likely to fit each group's current reading development. If necessary, use the chart on the previous page to help you select the appropriate Standard.

- Photocopy the relevant Standard Criteria assessment chart for each child in the group and, for each child, look at the criteria in detail and tick any criteria that you are confident they have already attained.

- Prepare for the assessment by selecting a book at the appropriate level – this should be a book which you are confident the children can all tackle, but which they have not seen before. Look at the criteria which you want to focus on in the assessment, and use these criteria to prepare questions to ask the children during the assessment.

- Gather the group together and ask them to read part of the chosen book. Sample their reading so that you can assess their word-reading skills and then talk to them about their understanding of the text in order to assess their comprehension.

- Against each of the remaining criteria, put a tick if a child has achieved it, a cross if they have not achieved it, and a dot if the child is 'almost there'.

- Count up the number of ticked criteria and use the box at the bottom of the Standard (for Standard 1 upwards) to make a judgement. As well as showing whether a child is Developing, Secure or Advanced against expectations, the judgement indicates the best Oxford Level for a child to be reading at.

Please note: although the criteria in each Standard are set out in broadly hierarchical order, this is only a general guide – children will not necessarily achieve the skills in the order presented – so it is important to consider and assess each criterion on its own merits regardless of where it appears on the Scale.

On-going, formative assessment

Using the records of individual children's assessments, marked on the *Oxford Reading Criterion Scale* assessment charts, you can plan future teaching. The criteria marked with a dot are thosewhich children are closest to achieving, and it makes sense to focus on these skills first. The criteria marked with a cross represent the skills which children are furthest from acquiring (look carefully at these, as they may include skills from further down the *Oxford Reading Criterion Scale* which need detailed revision and practice, as well as 'higher' skills which children have not yet begun to acquire). It is important to share next steps explicitly with the child so that they know exactly what their targets are and what they need to do to make progress in the short term and over the longer term. Once a child's next short term targets have been agreed, you can carry out on-going, formative observation and assessment during guided or independent reading sessions and record evidence of any criteria which are achieved between formal assessments.

Oxford Primary Reading Assessment

This publication provides detailed guidance on the Oxford Levels, the *Oxford Reading Criterion Scale* Standard Charts for the whole school (Pre-reading through to Standard 7) and correlation between Oxford Levels, Oxford Reading Criterion Scale Standards and all UK curricula.

For more information visit: **www.oxfordprimary.co.uk**

Oxford Reading Criterion Scale

Pre-reading Standard: Early Years

The Pre-reading Standard supports the observation and recording of early reading behaviours, listening and oral language skills. It is designed to help teachers evaluate children's pre-school experiences so that they can best meet the needs of the whole class.

Children whose experience of reading and language is good prior to starting school will readily demonstrate many of these behaviours and you will be able to teach, observe and assess these children against Standard 1 fairly quickly. Other children will need more exposure to books and language before they are ready for the more formal teaching of reading to begin.

Key to Reading Skills

READ = word reading and general reading behaviour

R = recall and retrieval

E = exploring the author's language and point of view

A = analysis of structure and organization

D = deduction and inference

Children at the Pre-reading Standard will be able to explore, talk about and identify letter sounds in words in books at Oxford Levels 1 and 1+.

PRE-READING STANDARD: Early Years		
Name:	**Date:**	
No.	**Criteria**	**Evidence?** (✔, ✗, ●)
1	Can hold books the right way up and turn the pages. (READ)	
2	Handles books carefully. (READ)	
3	Shows curiosity about books and chooses to look at books independently. (READ)	
4	Is beginning to distinguish between sounds in words, particularly initial letter sounds. (READ)	
5	Can recognize familiar words and signs such as their own name, advertising logos, other common words (e.g. 'mum' or 'dad'). (READ)	
6	Listens attentively to stories and other texts as they are read aloud (at an age-appropriate interest level). (READ)	
7	Can gain simple meaning from texts using illustrations, when not yet able to read the text itself. (D)	
8	Is beginning to talk about texts, e.g. stating simple likes/dislikes. (E)	
9	Shows curiosity about content of texts, e.g. may begin to discuss content and answer basic questions about a story (How? Why?). (D)	
10	Is beginning to recognize language patterns in stories, poems and other texts, e.g. repeated phrases, rhyme, alliteration. (A)	
11	Can explore and experiment with sounds and words. (READ)	
12	Can identify initial sounds in words. (READ)	
13	Can identify objects that begin with the same sound, e.g. table, tiger, tap. (READ)	
14	Can retell an event in a story or information from a non-fiction text (may only be brief). (R)	
15	Is beginning to draw on the knowledge of familiar stories/story structures to make predictions about unfamiliar stories, e.g. suggest how a story might end or what a character might do next. (D)	
16	'Pretends' to read familiar books, drawing on memory, language patterns and illustrations as prompts. (READ)	
17	Knows that text runs from left to right and top downwards in English. (READ)	
18	Is beginning to hear and identify where sounds appear in words. (READ)	

Standard 1: Reception/Primary 1

Standard 1 can be used during both formal and informal observations of children as their learning progresses through Reception/Primary 1. A review of the evidence gathered and a summative assessment of each child is recommended once a term.

By the end of Reception/Primary 1, children should be able to:

- handle books correctly,
- listen to stories and other texts read to them attentively,
- talk about familiar books confidently, including key characters, settings and events,
- use words and illustrations to gain meaning from stories and information books,
- read most common CVC words automatically,
- sound and blend words containing taught vowel and consonant digraphs,
- retell a known story in the correct sequence,
- find information to help answer simple questions,
- make simple predictions about stories and information books.

Children are expected to be a Secure Standard 1 – reading at Oxford Level 3 – by the end of Reception/Primary 1 in order to meet national expectations at the end of Key Stage 1.

NOTE: Children who can accurately, fluently and consistently read all the Reception Year GPCs and common exception words should be moved on to the National Curriculum Year 1 programme of study for word reading. However, they may still need further development of the wider reading skills outlined in Standard 1 below.

No.	Criteria	Evidence? (✔, ✗, ●)

Standard 1: Reception/Primary 1

Name:	Date:	

No.	Criteria	Evidence? (✔, ✗, ●)
1	Can distinguish between a word, a letter and a space. (READ)	
2	Can understand the terms: book, cover, beginning, middle, end, page, word, letter, line. (READ)	
3	When prompted, can use illustrations to support talk about what is happening in a text and to predict what might happen next. (D)	
4	Can sequence the important parts of a story that is known to the reader in order. (R)	
5	Can use developing GPC knowledge to sound and blend simple VC and CVC words. (READ)	
6	Is able to read some words from the YR high frequency word list. (READ)	
7	Can state simple likes/dislikes about familiar texts. (E)	
8	Can talk about the main points/key events in a text, e.g. main story setting, events, principal character. (R)	
9	Knows that information can be retrieved from different sources such as books, posters and computers. (R)	
10	Knows a wider range of GPCs and can sound and blend to read most CVC words (including words with double letters, e.g. bell, hiss). (READ)	
11	Can point to a full stop in text. (READ)	
12	Can retell familiar stories with growing confidence. (R)	
13	Is beginning to blend adjacent consonants in words in a range of combinations: CVCC CCVC. (READ)	
14	Can recognize language patterns in stories, poems and other texts, e.g. repeated phrases, rhyme, alliteration. (A)	
15	Can read words with consonant diagraphs: ch, sh, th, ng. (READ)	
16	Can read most of the YR/P1 high frequency word list. (READ)	
17	Without prompting, uses words and illustrations together to gain meaning from a text. (R/D)	
18	With support, can find information to help answer simple, literal questions. (R)	
19	Can read words with some vowel digraphs e.g. /ai/ /ee/ /igh/ /oa/ /oo/. (READ)	
20	Can talk about main points or key events in a simple text. (R)	
21	Is beginning to make predictions based on titles, text, blurb and/or illustrations. (D)	
22	Can read almost all the YR high frequency words. (READ)	
23	Knows the function of full stops when reading and shows this in their reading aloud. (READ))	
24	Can read most common CVC words automatically, without the need for sounding and blending. (READ)	
25	Can confidently sound and blend words containing taught vowel and consonant digraphs and some words with adjacent consonants. (READ)	
Total		

Assessment score

0–5 ticks = not yet working at this Standard; review against Pre-reading Standard 6–12 ticks = **Developing** (Oxford Levels 1+/2) 13–19 ticks = **Secure** (Oxford Level 3)	20–25 ticks = **Advanced** (Oxford Level 4) Assessment point: children with 22 or more ticks may be assessed against Standard 2.

Hero Academy and the Scottish Curriculum for Excellence

Hero Academy has been written by leading children's authors and rigorously developed by literacy and phonics experts to support the principles and practice of the Scottish Curriculum for Excellence (CfE) and the Literacy and English Experiences and Outcomes.

Challenge and enjoyment

Curriculum for Excellence: Literacy and English Principles and Practice states, 'Children and young people need to spend time with stories, literature and other texts which will enrich their learning, develop their language skills and enable them to find enjoyment.'[1]

Challenge and enjoyment are at the heart of **Hero Academy**. The 78 thrilling stories have been written by a team of top children's authors, with former Children's Laureate, Chris Riddell, and Paul Stewart as Series Editors. With a hugely appealing cast of heroes and villains set around a school for superheroes, the **Hero Academy** stories are full of action, adventure and humour. You will find many fun ideas in this teaching guide of how to introduce the series and tap into children's enthusiasm for superheroes through a range of engaging activities, including photocopiable masters (see pages 13–17, 28–34, and 125–156).

The combination of fine levelling and engaging stories with familiar characters in a fantastically appealing setting is a great way to hook children into the series and support them through small steps of reading progression.

Progression

Hero Academy features fully decodable, finely-levelled stories and follows a systematic synthetic phonics structure which offers small steps of phonic progression allowing children in Primary 1 the chance to practise and consolidate their phonics skills as they learn to become fluent and enthusiastic readers. Information about the phonic coverage and high-frequency words can be found on the back covers of each book and on the inside covers.

A detailed breakdown of the phonic content in each book can also be found on pages pages 43–47 of this handbook and information about the rigorous criteria behind each reading level is provided on pages 48–51.

For more on supporting early comprehension skills, see pages 19–21 of this handbook.

Personalisation and choice

Hero Academy is designed to be used flexibly in the classroom for independent, one-to-one, or guided reading sessions to inspire young readers.

The importance of developing the ability to learn independently, encouraging children to set their own targets and to take responsibility for their own learning is a core principle of *Curriculum for Excellence*. On pages 18–24 of this handbook, you will find suggestions of how to support children on their journey to becoming a reader. There are ideas of how to encourage children to discuss and reflect on their reading. See the *Reading journey record* photocopiable master (page 24).

---

[1] Scottish Government, HMIe, SQA, LTS; Curriculum for Excellence: Literacy and English Principles and Practice, https://education.gov.scot/Documents/literacy-english-pp.pdf

Also emphasized in *Curriculum for Excellence* is the importance of choice for children in the selection of reading books; **Hero Academy** is carefully structured in order that children can be given the opportunity to enjoy choosing a book from an appropriate level.

In this handbook, you will find advice for inspiring readers, support for independent and guided reading, comprehension, assessment and photocopiable masters.

Reading engagement

Hero Academy stories, with their colourful, digitally-generated pictures, appealing subject-matter, exciting stories and familiar characters, have been carefully developed with the importance of reading engagement, enjoyment and motivation in mind.

Accompanying the **Hero Academy** stories are a set of companions, perfect for hooking children into the series as they give more information about the heroes and villains along with extra story comic strips and things to make and do. They can be used as a springboard for writing activities, and can generate talk in pairs, groups or with the whole class.

Partnerships with parents

The importance of highlighting to parents the positive impact that they can have on their children's learning is explored in the Education Scotland publication, Engaging parents and families: *A toolkit for practitioners*. You can find more information about the importance of engaging parents in their children's learning and ideas of how to do so on pages 39–42 of this handbook. In addition, clear guidance for parents on how to support their child's reading can be found on the inside covers of each **Hero Academy** book.

Active learning and learning through play

In the *Activities to support reading (and writing)* section of this handbook (pages 25–34), you will find many ideas of how **Hero Academy** can be used flexibly to support active learning in the Early Years including role play activities, things to make and do, and how to use the series to promote collaborative and co-operative group work through group or guided reading.

This handbook also includes advice on setting up reading partnerships including resources such as a 'prompt' sheet (see page 34).

Assessment

Teachers in Scotland assess learning using a variety of approaches and a wide range of evidence. Ongoing assessment is a central part of everyday learning and teaching.

Hero Academy includes extensive and flexible support for the assessment of reading. Formative and summative assessment guidance is provided, based on the *Oxford Reading Criterion Scale*, to ensure teachers can monitor each child's progress and identify the skills they need to develop to be confident independent readers. For more information on assessment, see pages 102–113.

For support about encouraging self-reflection and giving feedback about reading as a two-way activity, see pages 35–38 of this handbook.

Hero Academy can help teachers in delivering the Literacy and English Experiences and Outcomes in Reading, and Listening and Talking as outlined in the table on the following page. Ideas of a range of follow-up activities to support children's writing are also provided throughout this handbook.

Scotland: Curriculum for Excellence: Literacy and English Experiences and Outcomes, Early Level

	Curriculum organizer	Experiences and Outcomes	Benchmarks
Listening and talking	**Enjoyment and choice**	• I enjoy exploring and playing with the patterns and sounds of language, and can use what I learn. LIT 0-01a / LIT 0-11a / LIT 0-20a • I enjoy exploring and choosing stories and other texts to watch, read or listen to, and can share my likes and dislikes. LIT 0-01b / LIT 0-11b • I enjoy exploring events and characters in stories and other texts, sharing my thoughts in different ways. LIT 0-01c	• Hears and says patterns in words. • Hears and says rhyming words and generates rhyme from a given word. • Hears and says the different single sounds made by letters. • Hears and says letter blends/sounds made by a combination of letters. • Participates actively in songs, rhymes and stories. • Chooses a story or other texts for enjoyment, making use of the cover, title, author and/or illustrator. • Engages with and enjoys watching, reading or listening to different texts, including stories, songs and rhymes, and can share likes and dislikes. • Engages with stories and texts in different ways, for example, retelling/re-enacting stories and/or using puppets/props.
	Tools for listening and talking	• As I listen and talk in different situations, I am learning to take turns and am developing my awareness of when to talk and when to listen. LIT 0-02a / ENG 0-03a	• Makes an attempt to take turns when listening and talking in a variety of contexts. • Listens and responds to others appropriately. • Asks questions and responds relevantly to questions from others. • Shares ideas with a wider audience, for example, group or class.
	Understanding, analysing and evaluating	• To help me understand stories and other texts, I ask questions and link what I am learning with what I already know. LIT 0-07a / LIT 0-16a / ENG 0-17a	• Asks and answers questions about texts to show and support understanding. • Makes simple predictions about texts.
	Creating texts	• Within real and imaginary situations, I share experiences and feelings, ideas and information in a way that communicates my message. LIT 0-09a • I enjoy exploring events and characters in stories and other texts and I use what I learn to invent my own, sharing these with others in imaginative ways. LIT 0-09b / LIT 0-31a • As I listen and take part in conversations and discussions, I discover new words and phrases which I use to help me express my ideas, thoughts and feelings. LIT 0-10a	• Talks clearly to others in different contexts, sharing feelings, ideas and thoughts. • Recounts experiences, stories and events in a logical sequence for different purposes. • Communicates and shares stories in different ways, for example, in imaginative play. • Uses new vocabulary and phrases in different contexts, for example, when expressing ideas and feelings or discussing a text.

	Curriculum organizer	Experiences and Outcomes	Benchmarks
Reading	**Enjoyment and choice**	• I enjoy exploring and playing with the patterns and sounds of language and can use what I learn. LIT 0-01a / LIT 0-11a / LIT 0-20a • I enjoy exploring and choosing stories and other texts to watch, read or listen to, and can share my likes and dislikes. LIT 0-01b / LIT 0-11b	• Chooses a story or other texts for enjoyment making use of the cover, title, author and/or illustrator. • Engages with and enjoys watching, reading or listening to different texts, including stories, songs and rhymes, and can share likes and dislikes.
	Tools for reading	• I explore sounds, letters and words, discovering how they work together, and I can use what I learn to help me as I read and write. ENG 0-12a / LIT 0-13a / LIT 0-21a	• Hears and says patterns in words. • Hears and says the different single sounds made by letters. • Hears and says blends/sounds made by a combination of letters. • Knows the difference between a letter, word and numeral. • Reads from left to right and top to bottom. • Uses knowledge of sounds, letters and patterns to read words. • Uses knowledge of sight vocabulary/ tricky words to read familiar words in context. • Reads aloud familiar texts with attention to simple punctuation. • Uses context clues to support understanding of different texts.
	Finding and using information	• I use signs, books or other texts to find useful or interesting information and I use this to plan, make choices or learn new things. LIT 0-14a	• Shows an awareness of a few features of fiction and non-fiction texts when using/choosing texts for particular purposes.
	Understanding, analysing and evaluating	• To help me understand stories and other texts, I ask questions and link what I am learning with what I already know. LIT 0-07a / LIT 0-16a / ENG 0-17a • I enjoy exploring events and characters in stories and other texts, sharing my thoughts in different ways. LIT 0-19a	• Engages with texts read to them. • Asks and answers questions about events and ideas in a text. • Answers questions to help predict what will happen next. • Contributes to discussions about events, characters and ideas relevant to the text. • Shares thoughts and feelings about stories and other texts in different ways. • Retells familiar stories in different ways, for example, role play, puppets and/or drawings. • Relates information and ideas from a text to personal experiences.

A breakdown of the Experiences and Outcomes and Benchmarks for each story at Early Level can be found online at: **www.oxfordowl.co.uk**

Hero Academy and the Foundation Phase Framework in Wales

Hero Academy has been developed in line with the Foundation Phase Framework and the National Literacy and Numeracy Framework in Wales. In particular, **Hero Academy** aims to support teachers in delivering the Language, Literacy and Communication Skills Area of Learning, with a focus on the Oracy and Reading strands.

Language, Literacy and Communication Skills

Strand: Oracy

Hero Academy features 78 engaging stories which are perfect for supporting the development of oracy skills. The Foundation Phase Framework emphasizes the importance of giving children opportunities to participate in active learning activities and in activities that encourage discussion. In the *Activities to support reading (and writing)* section of this handbook (pages 25–34), you will find many ideas of how **Hero Academy** can be used flexibly to stimulate discussion and support active learning. For example, through role play activities and opportunities to make and do. There is also support for how to use the series to support collaborative and co-operative group work through paired, group or guided reading.

Hero Academy provides many opportunities for children to express themselves creatively and imaginatively. For creative ideas of how to introduce the series to spark children's imagination and enthusiasm, see pages 10–17. The **Hero Academy** companion books can help provoke discussion, build anticipation and generate a 'buzz' around reading independently. For more information on the companions, see page 6.

The benefits of book talk to extend vocabulary and comprehension are emphasized throughout this handbook. You can find support for book talk in the form of question prompts on page 21. The questions provided on the inside cover notes of each of the **Hero Academy** books offer ideas to stimulate talk, encourage children to develop their thinking with open-ended questions and to express opinions, before and after reading.

Strand: Reading

The 78 thrilling **Hero Academy** stories have been written by a team of top children's authors, with former Children's Laureate, Chris Riddell, and Paul Stewart as Series Editors. With a hugely appealing cast of heroes and villains set around a school for superheroes, the **Hero Academy** stories are full of action, adventure and humour, and as such are designed to stimulate the interest and enjoyment of early readers.

The Foundation Phase Framework expects children to learn to blend and segment and to apply phonics strategies to their reading, together with a range of other reading strategies. **Hero Academy** features fully decodable, finely-levelled stories and follows a systematic synthetic phonics structure which offers small steps of phonic progression allowing children in Reception the chance to practise and consolidate their phonics skills as they learn to become fluent, accurate and enthusiastic readers. Information about the phonic coverage and high-frequency words can be found on the back covers of each book.

A detailed breakdown of the phonic content in each book can also be found on pages 43–47 of this handbook, together with information about the rigorous criteria behind each reading level.

The combination of fine levelling and engaging stories with familiar characters in a fantastically appealing setting is a great way to hook children into the series and support them through small steps of reading progression. The questions on the inside cover notes of the **Hero Academy** books, together with the comprehension support and Photocopiable Masters in this handbook, support the development of emerging comprehension skills. For more on supporting early comprehension, see pages 19–21 of this handbook.

Progression and assessment

The fine levelling of the **Hero Academy** stories supports children as they develop the skills they need to progress and build their reading stamina and fluency. **Hero Academy** includes extensive and flexible support for the assessment of reading. Formative and summative assessment guidance is provided, based on the *Oxford Reading Criterion Scale*, to ensure teachers can monitor each child's progress and identify the skills they need to develop to be confident independent readers. For more information on assessment, see pages 102–113.

For support about encouraging self-reflection and giving feedback about reading as a two-way activity, see pages 35–38 of this handbook.

Hero Academy can help teachers in delivering the Oracy and Reading strands of the Language, Literacy and Communication Skills Area of Learning in the Foundation Phase Framework as outlined in the table below. Ideas of a range of follow-up activities to support children's writing are also provided throughout this handbook.

		Language, Literacy and Communication Skills
Oracy	**Speaking**	Children are able to: • express what they like and dislike • talk about things from their experience and share information • use words, phrases and simple sentences • speak audibly • contribute to role play activities using relevant language • use a variety of questions, e.g. 'Who?', 'What ?', 'Why?', 'When?' and 'How?', to establish why things happen and to clarify understanding • use talk to create a storyline in symbolic/imaginative play
	Listening	Children are able to: • in simple terms, retell narratives or information that they have heard • answer 'Who?', 'What?', 'Where?' and open-ended questions relating to own experiences, stories or events • ask questions about something that has been said
	Collaboration and discussion	Children are able to: • exchange ideas in one-to-one and small group discussions, e.g. with friends • take part in activities alongside others, with some interaction

		Language, Literacy and Communication Skills

Reading	**Reading strategies**	Children are able to:
		• choose reading materials including books
		• understand that print carries meaning and is read left to right, top to bottom
		• discriminate between letters in a range of contexts
		• link and identify a growing number of spoken sounds to letters
		• recognize that words are constructed from phonemes (sounds) and that phonemes are represented by graphemes (written letters):
		  – orally blend combinations of known letters
		  – orally segment combinations of known letters
		• apply the following reading strategies with support:
		  – phonic strategies to decode simple words
		  – recognition of high-frequency words
		  – context cues, e.g. pictures, initial sound
		  – repetition in text
		• use one-to-one correspondence between written and spoken word
		• read simple words such as consonant-vowel-consonant words
		• read simple captions and texts recognizing high-frequency words
		• show an awareness of full stops when reading
		• show an awareness of the difference between stories and information texts
		• use pictures to aid understanding of text
		• make meaning from visual features of the text, e.g. illustrations, photographs, diagrams and charts

	Comprehension	Children are able to: • retell familiar stories in a simple way, using pictures to support • identify information from a text using visual features and words • relate information and ideas from a text to personal experience • predict an end to stories
	Response and analysis	Children are able to: • show an interest in books and other reading materials and respond to their content • follow texts read to them and respond appropriately.

A breakdown of the Language, Literacy and Communication Skills for each story at Foundation Phase can be found online at: **www.oxfordowl.co.uk**

Hero Academy and the Northern Ireland Curriculum

Hero Academy is a series of highly motivating books designed by reading and phonics experts to be used flexibly in the classroom. It can be used to support the development of communication skills, as outlined in the Northern Ireland Curriculum, and to support teachers in delivering the Statutory Requirements for Literacy and Language at Foundation Stage.

Encouraging a disposition to read

Hero Academy stories have been written by a team of top children's authors, with former Children's Laureate, Chris Riddell, and Paul Stewart as Series Editors. With a hugely appealing cast of heroes and villains set around a school for superheroes, children will love the **Hero Academy** stories because they are full of action, adventure and humour. The engaging 3D digital illustrations, exciting character-based stories, and first wordless books at Lilac Book Band, can help you to provide a rich literacy environment where children can choose appropriate stories, experience books independently and foster a disposition towards reading from the earliest stage.

Accompanying the **Hero Academy** stories are a set of companions, perfect for hooking children into the series as they give more information about the heroes and villains along with extra comic strip stories and things to make and do. They can be used as a springboard for writing activities, and can generate talk in pairs, groups or with the whole class. You will find many fun ideas in this teaching guide of how tap into children's enthusiasm for superheroes through a range of engaging activities, including photocopiable masters (see pages 10–17).

Reading in the Foundation Stage

Hero Academy is designed to be used flexibly to support different models of reading including independent, shared, one-to-one and group/guided reading sessions. The combination of fine levelling and engaging stories with familiar characters in a fantastically appealing setting is a great way to hook children into the series and support them through small steps of reading progression.

Independent reading

The first **Hero Academy** books at Lilac Book Band are wordless stories, which enable children to develop early communication, understanding and comprehension skills as well as simply choosing and experiencing books independently. From Pink Book Band, **Hero Academy** features fully decodable, finely-levelled stories and follows a systematic synthetic phonics structure which offers small steps of progression allowing children the chance to practise and consolidate their phonics skills and ensure they become fluent, accurate and enthusiastic readers who draw on a range of strategies. Information about the relevant phonic phase (as appropriate) and high-frequency words can be found on the back covers of each book.

A detailed breakdown of the phonic content in each book can also be found on pages 43–47 of this handbook, together with information about the rigorous criteria behind each reading level.

On pages 18–24 of this handbook, you will find information and ideas of how to support children on their journey to becoming a reader. There are ideas of how to encourage children to discuss and reflect on their reading. See the *Reading journey record* photocopiable master (page 24).

Emergent group/guided reading and modelled reading

You can find more information and support about how **Hero Academy** for early group or guided reading on pages 23, and 52–101.

The benefits of children in the Foundation Stage learning from adults modelling reading is well documented. For more about adult modelling reading area behaviours see page 11. Information about reading partners, can be found on page 27.

The importance of talking and listening

The importance of talk and other forms of communication in developing children's literacy and wider social skills is widely recognized. Talking and Listening is a core strand of the Language and Literacy Area of Learning and communication is a key cross-curricular skill in the Northern Ireland curriculum.

The **Hero Academy** engaging stories are perfect for supporting the development of communication skills. On the inside cover of each book there are ideas to stimulate talk and to encourage children to ask and answer questions and express opinions, before and after reading. For more information on the benefits of book talk, including question prompts, see page 21.

In the *Activities to support reading (and writing)* section of this handbook, you will find many ideas of how **Hero Academy** can be used flexibly to stimulate discussion, support active learning including role play activities and how to use the series to support collaborative and co-operative group work through paired, group or guided reading.

Assessment

Teachers in Northern Ireland assess learning using a range of techniques. **Hero Academy** includes extensive and flexible support for the assessment of reading. Formative and summative assessment guidance is provided, based on the *Oxford Reading Criterion Scale,* to ensure teachers can monitor each child's progress and identify the skills they need to develop to be confident independent readers. For more information on assessment, see pages 102–113.

For support about encouraging self-reflection and giving feedback about reading as a two-way activity, see pages 35–38 of this handbook.

Hero Academy can help teachers in delivering the Talking and Listening and Reading strands of the Statutory Requirements for Language and Literacy at Foundation Stage and Communication Skills as outlined in the tables below. Ideas of a range of follow-up activities to support children's writing are also provided throughout this handbook.

Statutory Requirements for Language and Literacy at Foundation Stage

	Literacy and Language: Foundation
Talking and Listening	Teachers should enable children to develop knowledge, understanding and skills in: Attention And Listening Skills through: • listening to a wide range of stories, poems, songs and music; • following instructions; • identifying environmental sounds; • repeating familiar phrases/sound sequences; • recalling sequence and detail. Phonological Awareness through: • responding to a steady beat; • identifying words in phrases and sentences; • identifying syllables; • identifying and generating rhymes; • identifying and manipulating phonemes. Social use of Language through: • observing modelled behaviours; • understanding non-verbal signals; • talking with adults and other pupils; • initiating and joining in conversations in pairs or groups; • working in different groupings; • adopting or assuming a role relevant to context. Language and Thinking through: • talking about experiences, pictures and stories; • talking about their work, play and things they have made; • naming; • recalling; • sequencing; • predicting; • asking and answering questions; • describing; • explaining; • sharing their thoughts, feelings and ideas with different audiences; • taking part/contributing to group oral language activities. An Extended Vocabulary through: • listening and responding to adults and peers; • an immersion in the language of books, both fiction and non-fiction; • focused experiences to introduce or generate vocabulary.
	Progression As pupils progress through the Foundation Stage they should be enabled to: • express themselves with increasing clarity and confidence, using a growing vocabulary and more complex sentence structure • initiate and sustain conversations with adults and peers in the classroom • retell stories, events or personal experiences in sequence with reasonable detail • answer questions to give information and demonstrate understanding • ask questions to find information or seek an explanation • offer reasons to support opinions given • listen with increasing attentiveness and for longer periods of time

A breakdown of the Statutory Requirements for Language and Literacy at Foundation Stage, and the Levels of Progression in Communication in Level 1, for each story can be found online at: **www.oxfordowl.co.uk**

Literacy and Language: Foundation	
Reading	Through modelled, shared and guided reading sessions pupils should be enabled to: • read with some independence; • read a range of texts including digital texts and those composed by themselves and others; • sequence stories in reasonable detail using appropriate language; • use word structure to develop reading; • develop auditory discrimination and memory; • develop visual discrimination and memory; • share a range of books with adults/other pupils; • know how to handle and care for books; • understand and use some language associated with books • select and use books for specific purposes; • develop concepts of print; • listen to a range of stories, poems and non-fiction texts read to them by adults/other pupils.
	Progression As pupils progress through the Foundation Stage they should be enabled to: • understand that words are made up of sounds and syllables and that sounds are represented by letters (phoneme/grapheme awareness) • recognize different types of text and identify specific features of some genres • use a range of reading cues with increasing independence and begin to self-correct • read on sight, some words in a range of meaningful contexts • begin to read with expression in response to print variations and punctuation • use extended vocabulary when discussing text, retelling stories or in their emergent writing • make links between personal experience and the text • make and give reasons for predictions • browse and choose books for a specific purpose.

Levels of Progression in Communication across the Curriculum: Level 1

Levels of progression	
Talking and Listening	In familiar situations, when listening to and responding to a range of stimuli, pupils can: • listen for information; • take on the role of someone else; • understand short explanations and simple discussions; • ask and answer questions for specific information; • use vocabulary from within their experience to describe thoughts and feelings; • talk about their experiences; • speak audibly to be heard and understood; • make eye contact and take turns whilst engaging in conversation.
Reading	Pupils can: • show understanding of the meaning carried by print, pictures and images; • understand that words are made up of sounds and syllables and that sounds are represented by letters; • use reading strategies; • read and understand familiar words, signs and symbols in the environment; • use visual clues to locate information; • use language associated with texts; • talk about what they read and answer questions

Order the story: *Cat Chase*

Cut out the pictures. Then put them in the right order to retell the story.

Make a moving picture

You will need: colouring pens, a lolly stick, sticky tape and scissors.

What you need to do:

1. Colour the background below and Jin.

2. Cut out Jin and stick him on to the lolly stick.

3. Cut along the thick black line between the two dots – get an adult to help you.

4. Push the stick behind the cut line. You can now make Jin fly through the air!

Name _____ Date _____

Say, blend, read, write

Say the sounds. Blend the sounds. Read the word. Then write the word in the box. The first one has been done for you.

t •	a •	p •		tap

s •	a •	t •		

p •	a •	t •		

P •	i •	p •		

a •	t •		

Match the letters

You will need: 4 different coloured pens or pencils.

What you need to do: Colour all the letters that make the same sound. Use a different colour for each letter. Say each sound as you colour it.

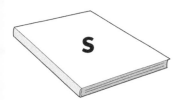 s   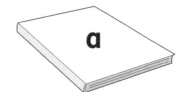 a   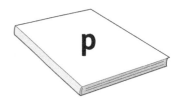 p

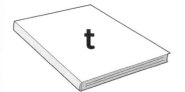 t   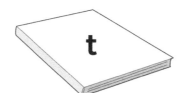 t    s

 t    p   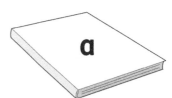 a

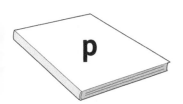 p   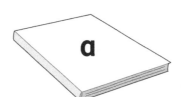 a    s

Oxford Level 1, Pre-Book Band Lilac B 🛡 Jin's First Day
© Oxford University Press 2018. Copying permitted within the purchasing school only.

Order the story: *Pip's Prank*

Cut out the pictures. Then put them in the right order to retell the story.

Complete the sentence

Choose the right word to finish the sentence:

mad   tip   tin   sad

It is a ___ ___ ___.

Mrs Molten is ___ ___ ___.

Pip is ___ ___ ___.

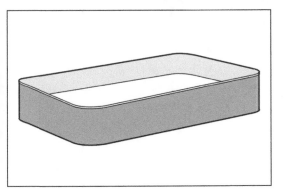

It is a ___ ___ ___ pan.

Name _____ Date _____

Slink's outfit

Label Slink's new superhero outfit.

Slink   cap   pom-poms   top   spots

Changing words

Read the word in the first column. Then change the middle letter/sound to make a new word. Read the words you have made. Tick or colour in the ones the ones that are real words.

Read the word	Add the new letter: a	Add the new letter: i
top	t__p	t__p
pot	p__t	p__t
sop	s__p	s__p

Read the word	Add the new letter: i	Add the new letter: o
pan	p__n	p__n
sat	s__t	s__t
Jan	J__n	J__n

Name _____ Date _____

Action words

Choose the right action word to finish the sentence:

picks   skids   runs   spins

	The rat _____.
	Slink _____.
	Slink _____.
	Magnus _____ up the rat.

Name _____ Date _____

Lasso words

Lasso the rhyming words together. The first one has been done for you.

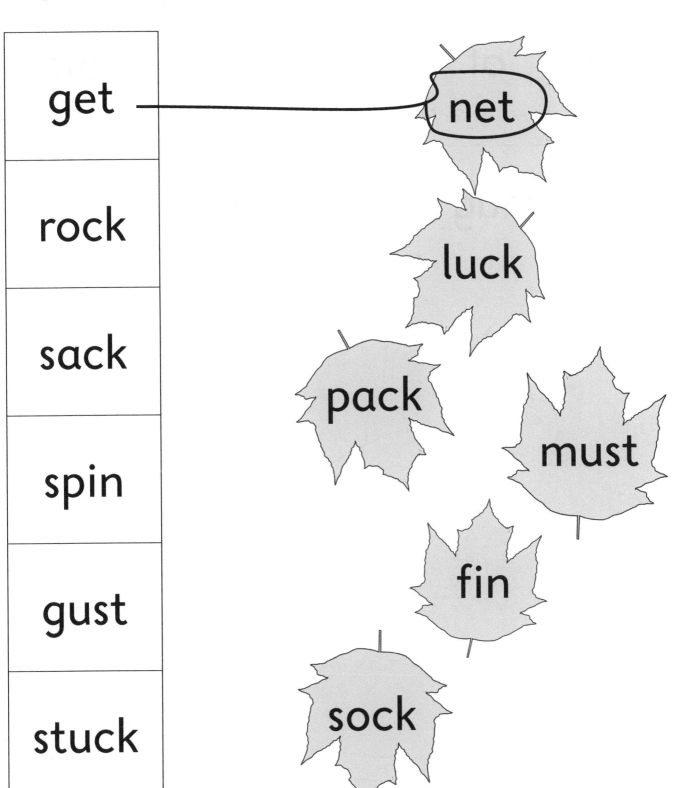

get
rock
sack
spin
gust
stuck

net

luck

pack

must

fin

sock

Name _____ Date _____

Make the sentence

Cut out the words. Then reorder the words to make a sentence.

Jin	of	a	gets	big

mug	hot	lemon.

Silly sentences

Read the sentences below carefully. The sentences look similar but only one makes sense. Circle the sentence that makes sense.

Can I help?	Cat I help?
Go and get the mop.	Go and get the mitt.
Miss Baker has a pit of hot cod.	Miss Baker has a pot of hot cod.
Ben sits the bin and drops the pot.	Ben hits the bin and drops the pot.
Ben gets rid of the mess.	Ben gets rod of the mess.

Jin's actions

Read the action words/phrases from the story *Jin Lifts Off* and then draw a picture from the story to match.

lift off	
ducks and dips	
twists	
six spins	
land on the box	

How many runs?

Read the sentence and then write the number of runs each superhero got in the box.

Sentence	Number of runs
Ben is fast and gets seven runs. 	_____
Pip jogs and gets six runs. 	_____
Jin bats and cannot hit it. 	_____

Name _____ Date _____

Machine name generator

Match the first part of the word to the second part to make up some new names for Ben's machine. Write the word and then read it. The first one has been done for you.

First part	Second part	New name
Zip	bot	Zipbot
	zig	
	zag	
	buzz	
Zig	skid	
	quick	
	bump	
	spin	

Choose your favourite name, and draw a picture of your machine on another piece of paper.

Mixed up sentences

Put these sentences in the order the events happen in the story. The first and last sentences have been done for you.

Pip cannot stop the liquid.	The liquid runs on the desk.	Pip mops up the mess.
Pip adds lots of liquid.	The liquid fizzes.	Add six drops of red liquid.

Add six drops of red liquid.		
		Pip mops up the mess.

Name _____ Date _____

Matching pairs game

Cut out the word cards. Put them face down on a table and mix them up. Then turn over two word cards and read the words aloud. If they are the same, you keep them. Play with a partner: who has the most pairs? Play by yourself: how long does it take you to find all the pairs?

that	this	then	them
that	this	then	them
we	me	be	with
we	me	be	with
back	off	no	I
back	off	no	I

Rhyming words

How many words can you spell that rhyme with these words from the book? Write them in the boxes.

Word from the book	Rhyming words
drink	
dash	
ping	
lunch	
that	

HERO ACADEMY

Match words to the picture

Match the words from the story to the picture. Draw a line from the correct word to the correct picture.

three	
tail	
coat	
cloak	

Name _____ Date _____

Dance moves

Complete each sentence using these words from the story.
Write the words in the spaces below.

floats	spins	fast
taps	twists	trips

Jin _____ up.

Ben is too _____.

Pip _____ up.

Slink _____, _____ and _____.

Name _____   Date _____

Two syllable words

Match the word part from each column to make a word from the story. Write the words you have made under the right picture. One has been done for you.

gar	nus
sweet	nip
Tur	et
Mag	den
pock	corn

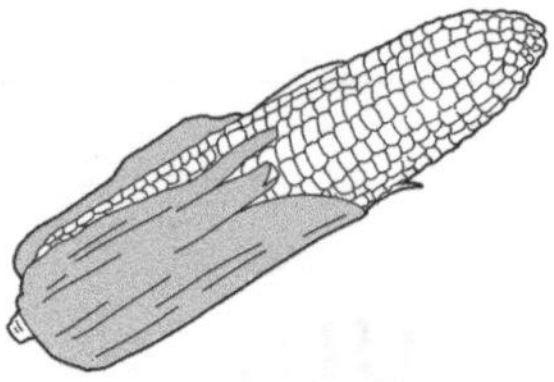

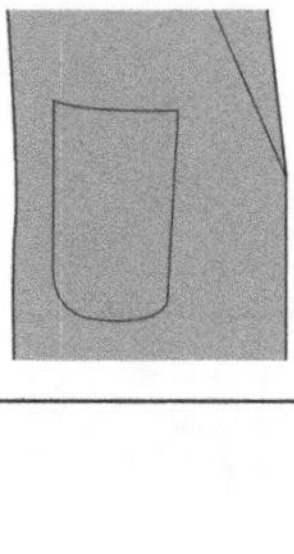

pocket

HERO ACADEMY

Name _____   Date _____

Mrs Butterworth's cook book

Read the list of zoom foods below. Choose 3 zoom foods each for Ben, Pip, and Slink and write them in the cook book.

eggs	toast	crisps	leeks	nuts
mash	carrot	garlic	lemon	pumpkin
fish	cheese	radish	mushroom	banana

Zoom food for Jin

1. *beetroot*

2. *turnip*

3. *popcorn*

Zoom food for Ben

1.

2.

3.

Zoom food for Pip

1.

2.

3.

Zoom food for Slink

1.

2.

3.

Name _____ Date _____

A powerful storm

Pip, Jin and Slink are stuck in a powerful storm. Draw a picture of what they can hear and see, and label it. Use the words in the boxes to help you.

Thunder crashes.	Pip is skidding.
The tree cracks.	The lightning flashes.

Match sentences to the pictures

Match the sentences to the pictures. Draw a line from the correct sentence to the correct picture.

Ben is not sure of the mixture.	
Ben spoils it with too much powder.	
The mixture splashes on Mrs Molten.	
Ben has to mix a cure.	
Mrs Molten gets down the ladder.	

Name _____ Date _____

Speech bubble

Teacher notes

Photocopy the speech bubble below (one per child) and cut out. If possible, laminate the speech bubbles for permanent use in guided reading or one-to-one sessions.

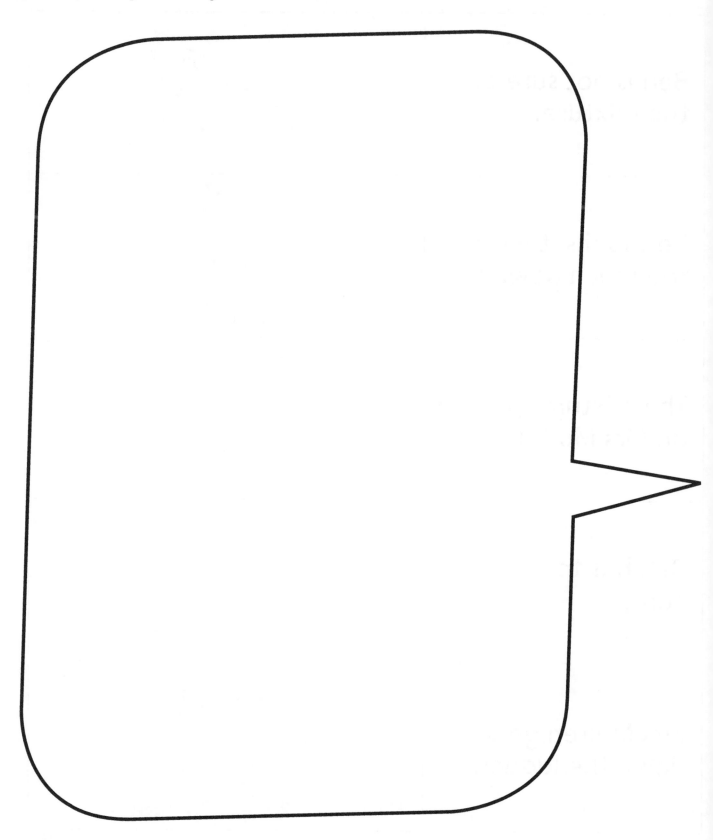

Name _____ Date _____

Magnifying glass

Teacher notes

Photocopy the magnifying glass below (one per child) and cut them out – make sure you cut out the 'lens' so children will be able to see through the middle. If possible, laminate the magnifying glasses for permanent use in guided reading or one-to-one sessions. Once laminated, you could use a whiteboard marker to write the focus tricky word/GPC on to the handle as a visual reminder.

Thought bubble

Teacher notes

Photocopy the thought bubble below (one per child) and cut out. If possible, laminate the thought bubbles for permanent use in guided reading or one-to-one sessions.

Name _____   Date _____

Feelings fan

Teacher notes

Cut out the shapes below and, if possible, laminate them. Punch a hole in the bottom of each shape and use a paper fastener to secure them together so that you can use them in a fan shape.

happy

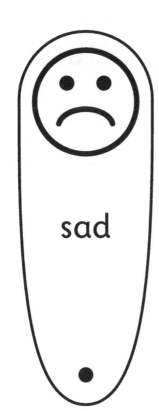
sad

cross/ angry

shocked/ surprised

tired

worried

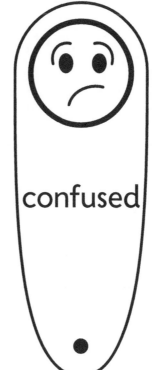
confused

upset

Super spotter

Teacher notes

Populate and photocopy the grid below (one per child), as directed in the Guided reading notes, with either the focus GPCs or the new tricky words (one per box/cell). Ask children to become 'super spotters'.

Be super spotters!

Name _____ Date _____

Splat mat

Teacher notes

Populate and photocopy the splats below (one per child), as directed in the Guided reading notes, with either the focus GPCs or the new tricky words (one per splat).

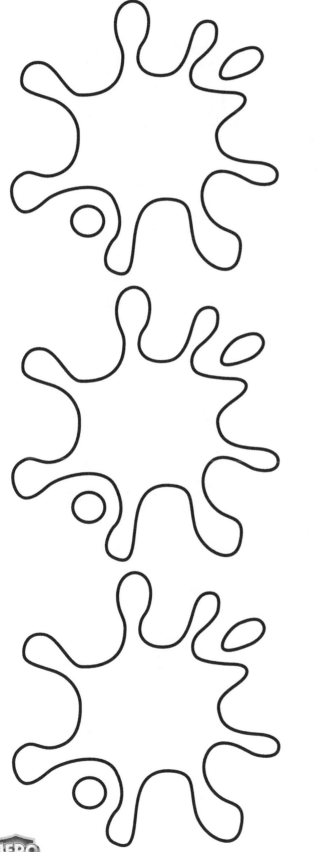
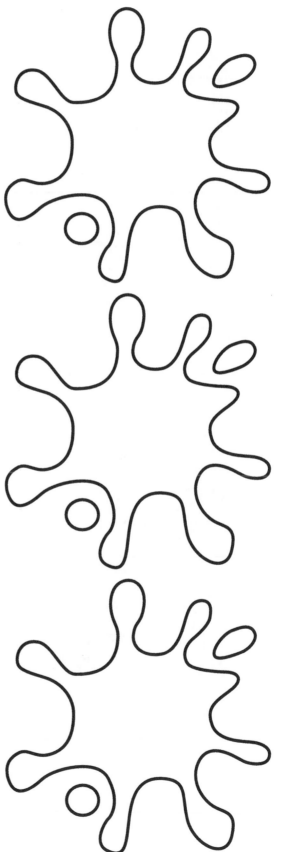

Name _____ Date _____

Character cards

Teacher notes

Photocopy the character cards below and cut them out. If possible, laminate the cards for permanent use in guided reading or one-to-one sessions to remind children of the characters' superpowers and to help with prediction.

Ben — (Sprint)

Pip — (Boost)

Jin — (Swoop)

Slink — (Combat Cat)